THE resilience WORKBOOK FOR WOMEN

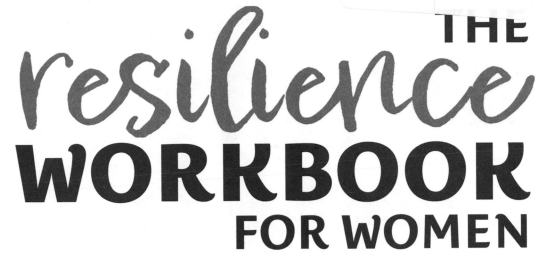

*A transformative guide to discover your **inner strength, conquer adversity,** and **achieve your goals***

Hope Kelaher, LCSW

ULYSSES PRESS

Published by:
Ulysses Press
PO Box 3440
Berkeley, CA 94703
www.ulyssespress.com

ISBN: 978-1-64604-505-1
Library of Congress Control Number: 2023932778

Printed in the United States by Sheridan Books Minnesota
10 9 8 7 6 5 4 3 2 1

Acquisitions editor: Claire Sielaff
Managing editor: Claire Chun
Editor: Renee Rutledge
Proofreader: Joyce Wu
Front cover design: Justin Shirley
Interior design: what!design @ whatweb.com
Artwork: leaves © Liashenko Iryna/shutterstock.com
Layout: Winnie Liu

IMPORTANT NOTE TO READERS: This book has been written and published for informational and educational purposes only. It is not intended to serve as medical advice or to be any form of medical treatment. You should always consult with your physician before altering or changing any aspect of your medical treatment. Do not stop or change any prescription medications without the guidance and advice of your physician. Any use of the information in this book is made on the reader's good judgment and is the reader's sole responsibility. This book is not intended to diagnose or treat any medical condition and is not a substitute for a physician. This book is independently authored and published and no sponsorship or endorsement of this book by, and no affiliation with, any trademarked brands or other products mentioned within is claimed or suggested. All trademarks that appear in this book belong to their respective owners and are used here for informational purposes only. The author and publisher encourage readers to patronize the brands mentioned in this book.

CONTENTS

Introduction

WHY A RESILIENCE WORKBOOK FOR WOMEN?

In a post-pandemic world, the word "resilience" is used more widely than ever. Whether it is in regard to a community, an individual, the planet, or the economy, we have all heard "resilience" used to describe an ability to move forward, come back from a difficult time, or rebound from failure. Although we all seem to have a general sense of what it means to be resilient, there is not much information out there on how to grow, build, and maintain your own resilience. If you are like any human I know, myself included, you may find it especially difficult to channel your sense of resilience and push through difficult times of hardship. Although most of us make it through challenging times generally unscathed, some of us find ourselves the worse for wear than others. Why is this?

The Resilience Workbook for Women aims to provide an overview of the theory behind resilience, along with core exercises rooted in a variety of psychological paradigms that will help you find, grow, build, and sustain your inner strength to persevere through your next challenge. This workbook will draw from cognitive behavioral therapy (see page 35), positive psychology (see page 102), somatic therapy (see page 27), philosophy, and meditation to help you access your inner resilience and cope and adapt when life throws you curveballs.

Why *The Resilience Workbook for Women* versus a book for everyone? Good question. There is no doubt that all humans suffer from difficulties; however, a substantial amount of research shows that women experience more hardship compared to their male counterparts, as they are faced with more adversity over the life course. While the definition of "adversity" may be subjective for some, research suggests that rates of adversity for both men and women appear to be steady until adolescence, when it increases for girls and women as they encounter higher rates of sexual/physical violence, caretaking responsibilities of children and parents, and relational difficulties with their partners.[1] Additionally, women continue to be adversely impacted by the gender gap, causing them to navigate issues such as work-life balance and unhealthy workplace climates. The truth is that resilience is an integral part of womanhood. *The Resilience Workbook for Women* aims to illuminate, excavate, and unlock the inner resilience that our female predecessors have bestowed within us. By utilizing the exercises discussed in this book, I hope you will not only survive the challenges you are currently facing, but

---

1 Monique Séguin, Guy Beauchamp, and Charles-Édouard Notredame, "Adversity over the Life Course: A Comparison between Women and Men Who Died by Suicide," *Frontiers in Psychiatry* 12 (August 10, 2021), https://doi.org/10.3389/fpsyt.2021.682637.

thrive. While no two human experiences are the same, this workbook aims to help you foster more resilience in circumstances such as physical and sexual trauma; loss; divorce; mental and physical illness; childbearing challenges; and natural disasters.

Some of you reading this workbook may be going through tremendous pain and suffering. You may have spent years or decades trying to overcome a specific issue. To manage this hardship, you may have tried many different remedies, from therapy to hypnosis to working out. Others may be evaluating and considering their capacity to foster a greater sense of resilience for the first time. Whatever reason brought you here today, it is important to honor and recognize that, however difficult, the road to survival and cultivating your resilience is worth it.

Before we begin, I will offer some initial reflections to keep in mind. First, you have likely purchased this book because you fundamentally believe in yourself. Even if that belief grows and shrinks at times, you know that it is there, and you have hope for yourself. The spark to endure and succeed is alive within you. Over the course of this journey, you may experience feelings of hope and empowerment, and possibly fear and loss. While there are no "right" or "wrong" feelings on this journey—I ask you to do one thing: do your best to hold onto hope. No matter what situation you are in, I promise it will change. My favorite mantra is *Nothing is permanent—not the good, not the bad.*

Second, working to build your resilience can be hard, and it may cause you to reevaluate many things in your life. It may result in you modifying or editing old narratives and creating new ones to fit your new life. This journey may call for you to consider a different finish line or to practice radical acceptance—a concept I will detail on page 57. As you move through the exercises in the workbook, do your best to maintain a nonjudgmental stance. You may be tempted to compare your suffering to others. While this may be okay some of the time, the hope is that you will use this time to focus on your own pain— no matter how big or small. Patience will be an important virtue to become familiar with because growth doesn't happen overnight. Remind yourself that you are not alone. Sure, your situation, experiences, and feelings are unique to you; however, out of the 7.753 billion people in this world, there is a likely chance that someone has an experience similar to yours. Get comfortable with ambiguity. Fear and hope come from the same place—the unknown. Before moving forward, take a moment to consider the following reflections that explore your willingness to grow:

What is the finish line or challenge you are working toward overcoming? How would you feel if it ended differently from how you imagine?

THE *resilience* WORKBOOK FOR WOMEN

How would you know if you were to be more resilient? What would that look like?

....

....

....

....

Can you name the scariest part(s) of this journey?

....

....

....

....

What are you most hopeful about in pursuing this journey?

....

....

....

....

We will revisit these questions toward the end of the workbook when you are closer to finishing your resilience building. As you move through the workbook, you may notice that some of your answers to the above questions may change over time. Note that there are no right or wrong answers. Remember that your journey toward resiliency is just that—*yours*.

* * *

Some of the exercises in this workbook may be more useful than others, depending on who you are and your current level of resiliency. Some of the exercises have been adapted and modified from experts in the field, while other exercises are derived from my own experiences with familial loss, bad breakups, aging, fertility, and physical and mental illness. While the hope is that this workbook will provide support for most of you reading it, it is important to acknowledge that everyone's experience is different. Resiliency, as this workbook will further explain, is influenced by several factors, such as social location, personality, age, faith, current coping styles, and childhood experiences. That said, there is no one-size-fits-all approach to a resilience journey, and as you move through this workbook, try to remain open to all the exercises. Experiment a bit and see if the information and exercises work for you—if they don't, then no pressure. Perhaps they may be helpful to someone else. Remember, what we don't know, we don't know.

My motivation for writing this book is twofold. A large part stems from my work as a social worker and psychotherapist in New York City. In my professional role, I witness resilience every single day—even in those who appear to be experiencing the greatest depths of despair. I believe that regardless of how hopeless a situation appears, resilience can be channeled and unearthed from within. I have had the privilege of working with individuals and families who have experienced severe trauma, displacement, loss, and betrayal grow capacity to manage life's toughest challenges and find fulfillment. The most rewarding part of my work is having the privilege to see someone's resiliency grow and manifest itself so that the individual can have a more meaningful and happier life.

The second motivation for writing this workbook stems from my own personal experiences with resilience. A few months ago, around the two-year anniversary of the start of the COVID-19 pandemic, a good friend and colleague commented on how surprised she was that I was "still standing." I chuckled and said, "What else did you expect?" The truth is that this friend had witnessed the unfolding and folding of my life over the past four years along a plethora of emotional experiences—ranging from parental loss, a partner's midlife mental health crisis, a separation, living alone during the pandemic, the ambiguous loss of fertility, and now, managing and coping with my significant other's bout with kidney cancer. While I can't say that the last four years of my life have been easy, I never once doubted that I would still be standing. In fact, the automatic thought I had after my friend's comments was, *I didn't even think I had a chance to give up!* Even in my darkest moments—moments of terror, sadness, and hopelessness—I just knew deep in my core that I had to keep on going. Upon reflection, I now know that part of that sensation was my need to survive, and the other part was resilience.

HOW TO USE THIS BOOK

Each chapter ahead will include some research on resilience as it applies to challenges that women face, such as loss, mental illness, physical illness, fertility, relational difficulties, and trauma. While this book covers a range of topics, it will by no means encompass all the adverse experiences women encounter. However, the variety of exercises related to strengthening your resilience can ideally be adapted and used as tools for whatever challenge you are experiencing.

Last, the workbook will include case scenarios based on case examples or the narratives of others. Note that all names and other identifying information have been changed to protect individuals' identities. While my hope is that you will find the tools you gain in this workbook to be useful to you, it is by no means a substitute for therapy and its intent should not be to *solve or fix* your situation, but for you to reflect upon and enhance your current resiliency skills and incorporate new ones into your tool chest. Last, I want to note that I do not proclaim this workbook to be revolutionary or to be a silver bullet to fix your problems. Consider it a reflective guide for you to build, flex, and strengthen different muscles while building your resilience.

Chapter 1

WHAT IS RESILIENCE REALLY?

Dating back to the mid-seventeenth century, the term "resilience" is widely used and can have multiple meanings. Derived from the Latin verb *resilire*, which means to "jump back or recoil," the word "resilience" became more widely used after English philosopher Francis Bacon likened its essence to a "round orb of air" that bounces as a ball would upon being thrown against a wall.[2] In Bacon's estimation, the use of resilience is synonymous with both the ball rebounding, or coming back, and resonating, meaning that when it hits the wall it has an impactful force.

The Oxford English Dictionary (OED) has expanded on Bacon's description of resilience and today defines it as "the capacity to recover quickly from difficulties; toughness; the ability to resist being affected by a misfortune, shock, illness, etc.; robustness, adaptability."

According to resilience researchers, a missing component of the OED's definition of resilience is not only your capacity to bounce back and withstand the hardship, but to repair yourself and come back even better after a difficult time.[3] For some, this definition of resilience means picking yourself up by your bootstraps and soldiering on; for others it may mean reconstructing a newer narrative and being okay with a different outcome. For resilience is not only about the comeback story and having a satisfactory quality of life but moving forward and not dwelling on the negative aspects of the experience.[4]

According to the National Scientific Council on the Developing Child, resiliency has a common cluster of features that include the following:

---

2 Danilo A. Caputo, "Shakespearean Resilience: Disaster & Recovery in the Late Romances," UC Irvine, 2020, https://escholarship.org/uc/item/61f0s5zm.

3 National Scientific Council on the Developing Child, "Supportive Relationships and Active Skill-Building Strengthen the Foundations of Resilience: Working Paper 13," Center on the Developing Child at Harvard University, 2015, https://developingchild.harvard.edu/wp-content/uploads/2015/05/The-Science-of-Resilience.pdf; Cheryl M. Bradshaw, *Resilience Workbook for Teens: Activities to Help You Gain Confidence, Manage Stress, and ... Cultivate a Growth Mindset* (Oakland, California: New Harbinger Publications, 2019); Steven J. Wolin and Sybil Wolin, *The Resilient Self: How Survivors of Troubled Families Rise above Adversity* (New York: Villard Books, 1994).

4 Julio F. Peres et al., "Spirituality and Resilience in Trauma Victims," *Journal of Religion and Health* 46, no. 3 (January 6, 2007): pp. 343–350, https://doi.org/10.1007/s10943-006-9103-0.

1. The capacity to adapt successfully to challenges that threaten your function, survival, or growth.
2. The ability to avoid negative behavioral and physiological changes in response to stress.
3. The ability to resume positive functioning at normal levels following exposure to an adverse event.
4. The degree to which you experience dysregulation, shock, or disturbance following an adverse event.
5. The ability to adapt to stress, trauma, and long-term forms of adversity.

At its essence, resilience is a positive, adaptive response to an adverse situation. Hence, it makes sense that the lack of or limited resilience can increase the risk of developing psychiatric disorders such as post-traumatic stress disorder (PTSD), major depressive disorder (MDD), and chronic anxiety.[5]

EXERCISE

Just as the journey of resilience differs from person to person, the definition and function of resilience does as well. Take a moment to reflect upon your definition of resilience:

In your experiences with hardship, has it been harder to bounce back in general or do you happen to get stuck in negativity around the situation?

EXERCISE

Imagine you are holding a red rubber ball. This ball represents your resilience. It has been tossed against a wall a million times. It keeps on coming back. Maybe it returns at a different angle, but you ALWAYS catch it. Imagine you throw this red rubber ball against a brick wall with force. You smash all those

---

5 Stephan Maul et al., "Genetics of Resilience: Implications from Genome-Wide Association Studies and Candidate Genes of the Stress Response System in Posttraumatic Stress Disorder and Depression," *American Journal of Medical Genetics Part B: Neuropsychiatric Genetics* 183, no. 2 (October 4, 2019): pp. 77–94, https://doi.org/10.1002/ajmg.b.32763.

THE *resilience* WORKBOOK FOR WOMEN

feelings that you have been holding. It feels good. It feels cathartic. Imagine the power within you, imagine the force with which it returns. Imagine the resistance/resilience you feel in that red rubber ball. That push/pull. Those momentary doubts that it will return. And maybe to your surprise it bounces right back at you, and you catch it.

How does the rebound feel? Can you handle the push and pull, or is too much? In the image you see of yourself tossing the ball, do you catch it every time? Notice what happens to your body. Do you notice if your feet start to move in sync with the ball? Do your arms and hands start to anticipate catching the ball?

The muscle memory developed from tossing this ball is quite like resilience. The more opportunities you take to practice overcoming a challenging circumstance, the easier it will be for you to bounce back and move forward.

NATURE VS. NURTURE

While practice and exposure to adverse experiences is helpful in building resiliency, a growing body of research indicates that environment and genetics also play a role. On a biological level, our road to resiliency starts in the womb. Epigenetics—the study of how your behaviors and environment can cause changes that affect the way your genes work without changing your DNA sequences—is showing us how the experiences of our parents impact us on a genetic and neurobiological level. So far, the research overwhelmingly indicates a correlation between maternal stress and the outcomes of a child, even into their adulthood.[6]

For instance, epigenetic research indicates that if a mother experiences trauma or stress during pregnancy, toxic stress hormones such as cortisol, a stress hormone, can impact the fetus. The current thinking is that while stress hormones trigger a response that promotes survival in utero, the genes that it turns on may not be ideal for survival outside of the womb. For example, toxic maternal stress experienced in utero may result in behavioral problems in childhood, which can lead to a variety of

---

6 Michael Ungar and Linda Theron, "Resilience and Mental Health: How Multisystemic Processes Contribute to Positive Outcomes," *The Lancet Psychiatry* 7, no. 5 (May 2020): pp. 441–448, https://doi.org/10.1016/s2215-0366(19)30434-1.

adverse outcomes as an adult, such as difficulties with school, peers, employment, etc.[7] Put simply, our DNA primes us for survival upon entry into the world by not only impacting our physical capacity but also by impacting how we relate to others and the world around us.

It is important to note that it is not all doom and gloom. Some experiences of stress may be helpful in creating resiliency. Consider the fact that we tend to be more resilient when we encounter a difficult challenge and come out on the other side. For instance, if we can anticipate a stressful experience based on past experiences, we tend to do better.

In terms of resilience training, it is important to understand the differences between the types of stress we encounter and how they contribute to our ability to bounce back. Researchers posit that we are typically more resilient when we encounter normative stress or adaptive stress, which are more manageable, than toxic stress.[8] See the nuanced differences between the types of stress below:

- **Normative Stress** is best defined as your essential response to danger and uncertainty. It is characterized by low to moderate increases in cortisol, which can be noticed in increased heart rate, shortness of breath, etc.

- **Adaptive stress** is a physiological state that has the potential to negatively impact brain functioning, but its severity can be mitigated by supportive positive relationships, community, and good physical health. An example of adaptive stress may be if you are pregnant and preparing for the birthing process. To prepare for the stress of childbirth, you may take some classes or hire a doula or have family provide additional support.

- **Toxic stress** tends to be overwhelming and can also be characterized as chronic. It appears to cause the prolonged and frequent activation of cortisol throughout the body. The stress takes longer periods to subside. Excessive or prolonged activation of toxic stress may lead to long-term changes in neurobiology; physical symptoms such as fatigue; autoimmune issues; and mental health concerns such as anxiety, depression, and PTSD. Physical health conditions and addictions may be seen as ways to cope with the current stress.

As mentioned earlier, it is always important to consider the context in which we experience stress and the resources, both physical and emotional, that are available to support us in moving forward. There appears to be a sweet spot between the types of stress we are exposed to and the growth of our own resilience. It seems that growth can occur when there is just enough stress (somewhere between the range of normative stress and adaptive stress) to be disruptive and to awaken the individual's need to

---

7 Iris M. Steine et al., "Maternal Exposure to Childhood Traumatic Events, but Not Multi-Domain Psychosocial Stressors, Predict Placental Corticotrophin Releasing Hormone across Pregnancy," *Social Science &Amp; Medicine* 266 (December 2020): p. 113461, https://doi.org/10.1016/j.socscimed.2020.113461; Nicole Bush et al., "Intergenerational Transmission of Stress: Multi-Domain Stressors from Maternal Childhood and Pregnancy Predict Children's Mental Health in a Racially and Socioeconomically Diverse, Multi-Site Cohort," *ISEE Conference Abstracts* 2022, no. 1 (September 18, 2022), https://doi.org/10.1289/isee.2022.p-1013.

8 Linda Mayes, MD, and Steven Southwick, MD, "Resilience in a Time of Uncertainty Presentation," Austen Riggs Center, September 10, 2022, https://education.austenriggs.org/content/resilience-time-uncertainty-understanding-toxic-stress -and-impact-covid-linda-c-mayes-md-and.

change aspects of their psychological, philosophical, or spiritual life.[9] It is then that the individual will have developed the resilience resources to continue forward.

The survivor of chronic or toxic stress, especially if exposed in utero or in early childhood, can find it difficult to bounce back or be as resilient as their peers who haven't had similar experiences. If you have experienced difficult things as a child, it may be helpful to visit the Adverse Childhood Experiences (ACEs) study, conducted by the Centers for Disease Control and Prevention (CDC), as some of these experiences can affect your mind, body, and emotions without your having a conscious awareness (aceresponse.org).[10] Having an awareness of your ACEs will be useful as you progress through this workbook, as it will be easier to choose resilience skills rather than your go-to protective patterns.

Knowing your protective patterns as you continue to build resilience is important. Many times, especially if you have suffered adversity and chronic stress in childhood, you may be primed to take actions in the moment that make you feel safe but have longer-term adverse outcomes. A person who may have experienced a violent childhood may respond to verbal aggression using physicality. For this person, the use of physicality may have helped them stay safe in the past and deal with danger, yet this reaction may not be ideal as it might lead to law enforcement involvement. Comparatively, a person who was not exposed to violence might simply walk away when confronted with verbal aggression, reducing their exposure to law enforcement. As demonstrated, reactions, unlike responses, can sometimes hurt important relationships and make you stuck, fearful, and burned out. It is important to note that, often, protective patterns are reactions, not responses, that likely result from chronic or toxic stress. The exercise below illuminates some of the common protective reactions that are often utilized, along with ways to modify your existing reactions so that they are more responsive. The hope is that once you are aware of your reactionary protective behavioral patterns you will have a stronger ability to choose how you respond. The following exercise will help you learn more about your protective behaviors.

EXERCISE

The protective behaviors listed below include some of the ways you (or someone else) might protect yourself in the event of a stressful situation.

- **Distrust:** You may be overly cautious of others and don't feel safe with them. You tend to lean into feelings of self-doubt, feeling like you are not smart enough.

- **Hypervigilance:** You may see potential danger everywhere. You experience constant anxiety and worry.

9 Mayes, MD, "Resilience in a Time of Uncertainty Presentation."

10 Centers for Disease Control and Prevention, "Adverse Childhood Experiences (ACEs)," last updated April 2, 2021, https://www.cdc.gov/violenceprevention/aces/index.html.

- **Hyper-caretaking:** You take care of others so much that you ignore your own needs. You may notice that you start to feel resentment and like a victim when you put other people's needs ahead of your own.
- **Avoiding:** When you ignore problems and hope that they will take care of themselves. You might use substances or maladaptive ways to numb out, such as overusing substances, eating too much, and spending too much.
- **Defending:** When you are compelled to prove you are right—even if it isn't helpful to your relationships. You respond to others and situations as though you were being judged or accused.
- **Attacking:** This may look or sound as though you are being mean to others. You maintain a stance of blaming and judging others and yourself.

As you move through this exercise, consider how each of these protective patterns is useful and how you react and respond to these protective patterns. Be honest with yourself and reflect on the questions for self-reflection:

1. How does this pattern help keep you safe?
2. How is this pattern good?
3. When you are distrusting, how do you hurt myself?
4. When you are distrusting, how do you hurt others?
5. How would you be helped if you were to become less distrusting?

Then ask yourself how you can be more responsive. If you need some ideas, review the list of ways to respond in a healthy manner:

- Consider taking a more compassionate stance toward the situation or person you are responding to. Examine the genesis of this mistrust. Is it rooted in the here and now?
- Practice mindfulness to slow down the negative thoughts. Orient yourself by telling yourself ways that you are safe. Consult with your support network to get different perspectives about your well-being. Notice what IS working in your life instead of what isn't.
- Try to employ the same compassion and empathy that you have toward other people to yourself. Can you help others while putting yourself as a priority? Can you help others become more independent so they can help themselves?
- What is the scariest part of the situation you are avoiding? Weigh the odds about that scary situation and see if they are likely to come to fruition. You can also set healthy boundaries.
- Maintain a stance of curiosity instead of defensiveness/protectionism.
- Can you empathize with the person and situation before you? Can you have authentically healthy boundaries and assert them?

Ask yourself how you react and if these behaviors would be different if you were more responsive. The aim of this exercise is to help you move toward more responsive ways to navigate hardship.

	SELF-REFLECTION OF PROTECTIVE BEHAVORS	HOW CAN I BE MORE RESPONSIVE?
DISTRUST	1. 2. 3. 4. 5.	
HYPERVIGILANCE	1. 2. 3. 4. 5.	
HYPER-CARETAKING	1. 2. 3. 4. 5.	

	SELF-REFLECTION OF PROTECTIVE BEHAVORS	HOW CAN I BE MORE RESPONSIVE?
AVOIDING	1. 2. 3. 4. 5.	
DEFENDING	1. 2. 3. 4. 5.	
ATTACKING	1. 2. 3. 4. 5.	

THE *resilience* WORKBOOK FOR WOMEN

Many times, we are unaware of how we engage in reactionary behavior until it threatens or compromises our livelihood, sense of self, or relationships. Consider the case of Jackie.

CASE SCENARIO

Jackie was a client in her mid-40s. She had been divorced a few years before coming to counseling and had two adolescent children. Jackie worked in the tech industry and was her family's financial provider. Up until recently, her job had been steady. At the time of her first visit, Jackie had been placed on a performance improvement plan—essentially her company's last-ditch effort to reach an agreement before termination—an event which completely disrupted Jackie's life and created a great deal of stress, as it would for anyone in this situation.

When we further explored the rationale for this improvement plan, we learned that the survival strategies that had helped her succeed in her industry as the daughter of immigrant parents were no longer helping her. Instead, those protective patterns/survival strategies—Jackie's spirit of competitiveness and her sense that someone was out to get her job—caused her to have interpersonal challenges with her colleagues that were now interfering with her work product. Once we examined the genesis behind Jackie's protective actions, we learned that Jackie had internalized messages about trusting others with her work. In fact, a message that Jackie had internalized from her father was literally *Trust no one*. In our sessions, she could hear her father's voice saying, "Everyone is out to get you." Of course, anyone receiving this message might be hypervigilant about their work and, subsequently, operate in a distrustful manner. While these strategies helped Jackie achieve great grades and entrance into a top-level college, they were not ideal for sustaining longevity in her career.

Our work together consisted of reframing some of these premises as well as exploring the legacies of intergenerational trauma that promoted the development of these patterns.

As soon as Jackie was able to reframe the narrative that she had inherited from her father that everyone was "not to be trusted" and maintain an open-minded stance with her colleagues, she was able to break these negative protective patterns and get off the performance improvement plan.

Jackie consistently had to work on self-talk around trust and be more mindful about her hypervigilance. Over time her efforts to reframe, practice mindfulness, and give others grace allowed her to approach her work differently. Today Jackie prides herself on her ability to collaborate with others, have transparent conversations with her colleagues, and maintain a stance of curiosity when met with a challenging experience.

To some extent, I imagine that we can all identify with an experience like Jackie's. We all have been primed to react to our experiences and environments until those reactions are no longer helpful. While appreciating how some of these protective patterns are informed by our lived experiences, I think it is important for us to understand our bodies' physiological response. Consider the work of Bessel van der Kolk, a psychiatrist, author, and researcher who focuses on traumatic stress. In his seminal piece of work *The Body Keeps the Score,* van der Kolk puts forth that our bodies unconsciously remember many of our positive and negative experiences and are constantly bombarded with messages to keep us safe. At times, that process impacts how we navigate the world.[11]

To that end, consider the diagram below demonstrating the physiological implications of stress reactions versus resilient responses. This visual representation modified from We Are Resilient™ Anticipatory Guidance Cards for Healthcare Providers (https://www.dovetaillearning.org) highlights the benefits of using more resilient, responsive reactions than protective, stress reactions. The diagram re-affirms the premise that until we are aware of our protective patterns, we tend to respond to stress automatically and risk making impulsive decisions. However, when we can reflect on our protective patterns and contemplate if that is the best way to react, we can become centered more quickly.

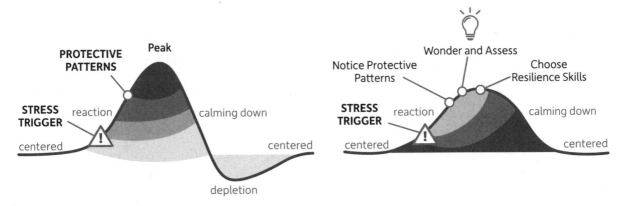

Although the world of epigenetics is simultaneously fascinating and daunting, it is also incredibly hopeful. While I've detailed how we are all influenced by our parents, intergenerational trauma, and gene expression, it is also true that we are all impacted by factors that exist in our environments. Have you ever wondered how two people experiencing the same situation could have different outcomes and life-course trajectories? For instance, why can one person seemingly overcome an adverse problem while another person in the same position may seem limited in their potential?

Research indicates that response to adversity goes beyond the science of epigenetics. There is a large amount of evidence that resilience is impacted by socioenvironmental factors, emotional regulation, solid social support, and positive familial relationships in childhood.[12] Resilience research spanning childhood and adolescence suggests that a critical component of resilience in our younger years is

---

11 Bessel van der Kolk, *The Body Keeps the Score: Mind, Brain and Body in the Transformation of Trauma* (UK: Penguin Books, 2015).

12 Deirdre Gartland et al., "What Factors Are Associated with Resilient Outcomes in Children Exposed to Social Adversity? A Systematic Review," *BMJ Open* 9, no. 4 (April 2019), https://doi.org/10.1136/bmjopen-2018-024870.

THE *resilience* WORKBOOK FOR WOMEN

building a close, supportive bond with a caregiver. At this point, you might wonder how your childhood experiences correlate to your resilience today. First, I believe it is vital to know where you came from to understand where you are going; second, the foundation of resiliency gets laid as soon as we are out of the womb. Some core features of resiliency, such as a sense of optimism, adaptation, and positive relationships, are primarily influenced by our caregivers.

Consider the case of Aerin, a 41-year-old cisgendered, multiethnic, heterosexual female living in NYC and working at a top corporate law firm.

CASE SCENARIO

Aerin initially came into therapy for treatment for anxiety caused by work-related stress, and a recent diagnosis of an autoimmune condition resulted in extreme fatigue that would sometimes stop Aerin in her tracks. This diagnosis was challenging for Aerin to manage as it impacted how she was feeling and, during a flare, impacted her work performance.

The loss of function was emotionally and physically hard for Aerin, a self-proclaimed over-functioner. Following her diagnosis, Aerin took a medical leave from her job. This was a challenging decision for Aerin, who had degrees from top schools and once prided herself on maximizing every spare moment she had on "personal growth." But faced with a new situation, Aerin was forced to make sense of this change and create a new meaning in her narrative.

At first, managing pain and disappointment proved to be especially hard for Aerin. Over time, it became easier for her to adapt and shift her perspective. After several sessions talking about Aerin's ailing grandmother—who had survived a Nazi concentration camp—Aerin started to recount some stories her grandmother shared with her when she was a small child. The stories focused on her grandmother's ability to hold optimism about the future despite the dire circumstances, showing her grandmother's ability to make sense of this experience and reframe why it had happened to her. Such stories offered Aerin a sense of hope—that even if she remained ill due to this autoimmune disorder and never returned to her job as a corporate attorney—she would be okay. If her grandmother could survive and endure such trauma and live a fulfilling life, she could too. After a few months, she decided to leave her corporate job and study functional medicine.

The example of Aerin is exceptional. Aerin's legacy of trauma and the role of epigenetics could have limited her ability to move forward with her life and create a new narrative. However, the fact that she internalized her grandmother's messages of optimism and hope allowed her to reframe her current situation and create a new path for herself.

Through Aerin and her grandmother, who created a different narrative as a result of their pain, we can see the importance and the benefit of having positive, close relationships with family and caretakers.

A good way to understand the development of resilience is to visualize a seesaw. When people have more protective/positive experiences and adaptive skills on one side, this counterbalances the adversity on the other side. The hope is that even when there is a heavy load on one side of the seesaw, there are enough positive experiences to tip the scale toward positive outcomes. Research suggests that no matter the source of hardship, we start to develop resiliency in early childhood.[13] As exemplified in Aerin's case, a primary ingredient is having at least one stable and supportive relationship that can provide scaffolding and protection from disruptions and hardships.

These relationships, if healthy, also help our younger selves develop core skills—such as the ability to plan, to monitor, and to regulate emotions and to adapt to different circumstances—that allow us to move through and overcome adversity.[14]

EXERCISE

Use this exercise to look back into your past. Who provided you with emotional, physical, or mental support when things got complicated? Consider the messages they offered to counter some difficult times in your life. Write down their messages on one side of the seesaw, and the challenges you were facing on the other. Consider those in your world now who may help counterbalance some of life's challenges. Add their messages and your current challenges to the seesaw.

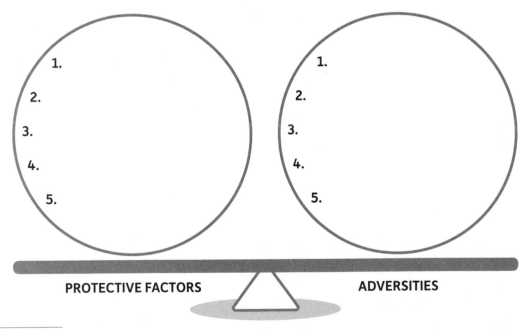

13 "Resilience," Center on the Developing Child at Harvard University, August 17, 2020, https://developingchild.harvard.edu/science/key-concepts/resilience.

14 "Resilience," Center on the Developing Child at Harvard University.

Notice those protective/empowering messages you received during your younger years. Are any of those messages still valid? Could you imagine reminding yourself of these messages from childhood when things become tough for you in the present? Are there any messages that you received in adulthood that may be helpful to remind yourself of when working through adversity?

EXERCISE

We are all the beneficiaries of another woman's strength. Reflect upon a woman or the women in your life you would like to emulate, whether they are biologically related or spiritually connected. Consider the direct and indirect messages of resilience you may have received. If this is a difficult exercise, consider a fictional or nonfictional person instead. Remember, this is for you, and there is no right or wrong answer.

....

....

....

....

What characteristics/features/life experiences of this person have helped build the foundations of their resilience?

....

....

....

....

....

If you could build your own female warrior, what traits would she inherit from the strong women in your life? Imagine what she would look like here. You can either draw or write down what you envision.

MEASURING AND MAKING SENSE OF YOUR OWN RESILIENCY

A LANDSCAPE VIEW OF YOUR RESILIENCY

When I ask my clients to reflect on their resiliency, they can often cite examples from their past—challenging moments when they overcame an adverse experience. Still, few can speak to their resilience on the day to day. Below, you will be able to evaluate your own resiliency using The Brief Resilience Scale, a tool used to assess one's ability to bounce back from hardship.[15]

EXERCISE

Evaluate your daily resiliency using the Brief Resilience scale below on a 5-point scale ranging from 1 to 5, with 1 being "strongly disagree" and 5 being "strongly agree."

If you are interested in obtaining the full scale along with instructions about scoring, visit the CD-RISC website at https://www.cd-risc.com.

---

15 Bruce W. Smith et al., "The Brief Resilience Scale: Assessing the Ability to Bounce Back," *International Journal of Behavioral Medicine* 15, no. 3 (September 2008): pp. 194–200, https://doi.org/10.1080/10705500802222972.

STATEMENT	STRONGLY DISAGREE	DISAGREE	NEUTRAL	AGREE	STRONGLY AGREE
1. I tend to bounce back quickly after hard times.	1	2	3	4	5
2. I have an easy time making it through stressful events.	1	2	3	4	5
3. It does not take me long to recover from a stressful event.	1	2	3	4	5
4. It is easy for me to snap back when something bad happens.	1	2	3	4	5
5. I usually come through difficult times with little trouble.	1	2	3	4	5
6. I tend to take a short time to get over setbacks in my life.	1	2	3	4	5
My Score (Sum ÷ 6)					

Now that you have completed this inventory, add all the numbers up and divide it by 6! That will give you your final score between 1 and 5. A higher score on this assessment correlates to higher levels of resiliency, but don't worry! Whether you selected all 1s or all 5s or somewhere in between, the purpose of this exercise is to assess your baseline of resiliency—know that it is not where you will likely end up if you move through this workbook and practice these exercises. The point is where you are *going* and how you *get* there.

ZOOMING IN: YOUR RESILIENCY MAKEUP

It is important to reiterate that while your environment and biology contribute to your resiliency, resiliency is not stagnant. We can all grow our resiliency; however, reflecting upon and assessing your baseline for the different types of resiliencies already within you can help you measure and determine where you need to focus your time. The three types of resiliencies are:[16]

NATURAL RESILIENCE

Natural resilience is what you were born with, which is impacted by your genes. Natural resilience is observed in your character and your personality. Those with natural resilience approach situations, even adverse ones, with enthusiasm, optimism, and an overall sense of positivity. Those who exude natural resilience typically see an opportunity, even in moments of crisis. While we all have a fraction of natural resilience when we are born—consider how young children approach the world with ease and wonder—most of us transition out of this general state as we face life's challenges and adapt. Interestingly, resiliency research indicates that there may be 71 candidate genes associated with resilience,[17] and that those with two long allele genes tend to cope better with extreme adversity than those with short alleles. As a result, resilience has a biological basis that is influenced by our circumstances.

ADAPTIVE RESILIENCE

Two truths of the human condition are that: 1.) we are all born with some degree of resilience, and 2.) we all experience some hardship resulting in *adaptive resilience.* Unlike natural resilience, adaptive resilience is born out of struggle. Consider the adage "When the going gets tough, the tough get going," the point being that adaptive resilience is something that is learned and results only from having had a hardship. As I mentioned earlier in the workbook, overcoming one obstacle allows many to develop the skills or muscles to persevere through the next challenge. Adaptive resilience means more than experiencing a challenge; it means working through it and making meaning. Through adverse experiences, your adaptive resilience allows for incremental adjustments anticipating future change (i.e., learning how to *roll with life's punches*.) Another component of adaptive resilience is that sometimes, when you have nothing more to give, you can and will seek/ask for support from your networks. We will talk more about this in future chapters of the workbook. Consider the case of Jane.

CASE SCENARIO

Jane was 23 years old when she was paralyzed from the waist down in a skiing accident. Before the accident, Jane described herself as an energetic, athletic recent college graduate who had embarked on a journey to New York City. As you can imagine, initially, the impacts

---

16 David Ogilvie, "The Three Types of Resilience," last accessed March 20, 2023, https://www.resiliencetraining.co.uk /the-three-types-of-resilience; MSc. Leslie Riopel, "Resilience Examples: What Key Skills Make You Resilient?," PositivePsychology.com, March 10, 2023, https://positivepsychology.com/resilience-skills.

17 Stephanie Cahill, Tarani Chandola, and Reinmar Hager, "Genetic Variants Associated with Resilience in Human and Animal Studies," *Frontiers in Psychology* 13 (May 2022), https://www.frontiersin.org/articles/10.3389/fpsyt.2022.840120 /full.

of this accident were catastrophic for Jane—not only would she have to relearn some major fundamentals, such as walking, but she would have to reconceptualize how she envisioned her life. Over time, with a lot of physical therapy, community support, and an upbeat attitude, Jane made meaning out of her accident. When she was ready, Jane could compete in the Paralympic Games and become a role model for others with similar experiences. In some ways, Jane's attitude toward what happened and her ability to reframe or change the narrative buoyed her resiliency.

EXERCISE

Assess your adaptive resilience. Can you identify past experiences or times when you had to work through a challenge and craft a new meaning out of that experience? Detail those experiences and the meaning you drew from them below.

....

....

....

....

....

RESTORED RESILIENCE

Restored resilience is the third type of resilience—the primary focus of this workbook. This type of resilience skill-building takes time and intentionality. Restored resilience is learned and builds upon our natural capacity.[18] To some extent, restored resilience is both having knowledge of resilience and being able to implement and build upon skills that support adaptive growth. Consider the case of Rachel, a former client who had experienced sexual trauma at the age of 15 years old. As a result of this trauma, Rachel suffered from PTSD symptoms ranging from anxiety, flashbacks, and intrusive thoughts. Through a lot of trauma counseling and some resilience strategies, Rachel eventually could mitigate some of these symptoms and adaptively cope with her experiences.

---

[18] MSc. Leslie Riopel, "Resilience Examples: What Key Skills Make You Resilient?"

Assess your own restored resilience. Can you identify past experiences or times when you have had to employ something you learned or a skill to work through a hard experience? Detail those experiences and the skills you employed below.

....

....

....

....

....

The best way to conceptualize the interplay between these three types of resilience is to consider them as energy tanks. When one of them runs low, the two other tanks can compensate. For instance, if someone has a lower natural resiliency tank but their adaptive and restored resiliency tanks are fuller, they will be better able to perform, function, grow, and be well in moments of crisis. If all three tanks are running on empty, then it is likely that one will be more vulnerable and have reduced functioning during a challenging event or adversity. When your resilience tanks run on empty, you may be more susceptible to feeling down, burned out, or depressed.

EXERCISE

Using the images below, shade in how full or empty your resilience tanks are now.

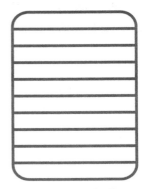

NATURAL RESILIENCE TANK **ADAPTIVE RESILIENCE TANK** **RESTORATIVE RESILIENCE TANK**

If you notice that one of these tanks is lower than another, take note, as this information will be helpful for you throughout the workbook. For instance, it may be beneficial to gauge if you need to focus on building your adaptive or restorative resilience. If you have a sense of this, you can identify and select which exercises in the workbook may be best to reach your goal.

But before we continue, I recognize various emotional triggers may come up for those reading this book. I further acknowledge that examining your current levels of resilience and unpacking some of the core components can be overwhelming. If this speaks to your experience, know that it makes complete sense, and this is a common experience when I explore the themes of resilience in my practice. Sometimes this happens if we tend to be more sensitive or anxious, and sometimes it happens if we avoid big feelings and push them down.

As you will find out, a large part of the resilience work is also becoming more aware of your thoughts and behaviors and regulating your feelings. Below are two mindfulness exercises aimed to help improve your mind-body connection. Having roots in somatic therapy, these exercises aim to help regulate your nervous system and build your capacity to feel your feelings better. Why is this important? For starters, feelings are our internal compass—they tell us where to go and how far. For instance, if you are very in tune with your emotions and, for example, you start to feel scared or anxious, you may change your behavior or move toward something that feels safer. As you will see in the upcoming sections, a large part of resilience is following the guidance of your internal compass and understanding how your thoughts are connected to your feelings and actions.

EXERCISE

Before you can acquire and internalize ways to regulate strong emotions/and or stress, it is crucial to know what is going on in your body. The exercise below will help you develop body awareness. This exercise asks you to slow down and witness your feelings, thoughts, sensations, movements, and behavioral responses to the people, places, and things around you. Remember, there are no right or wrong responses in this exercise.

Cue: Take a moment to review the exercise and the directions below. Once you have a sense of what the exercise entails, feel free to put down the workbook and your device. Then imagine suspending this moment as it allows you to take a second to tune in to your body.

1. Stop: You are pausing what you are doing right now.
2. Take stock: Notice what is happening to you in this very moment. Maybe you close your eyes. Become aware of the objects, the scents, and the sounds that are in your environment.

3. Track: Imagine doing a check-in of your body parts. Your head. Your arms. Your chest. Your thighs. Your calves. Your hands. Your feet. Ask yourself how these body parts are feeling. There is no judgment.

4. Stick with it: Stay in this moment. Sit in the same position. Stay present with the sensations in your body.

5. Repeat: Do this exercise again and see if you experience yourself differently.

Complete the following sentences.

1. Right now, I am noticing that my attention/focus is _____.

2. Right now, my body is experiencing _____.

3. Right now, my awareness is _____.

EXERCISE

While the above exercise assumes that you are good at identifying feelings and sensations within your body, it is very important to note that not everyone clearly understands the range of emotions. This exercise aims to help you better understand the range of emotions that you might experience. Examine the list of feeling words below. While it is not an exhaustive list, it is a good starting point for those who are less familiar with how their body feels. Having a sense for your feelings will be helpful in your resilience journey, as feelings often tell us where to go, what to do, and how to do it. Being in touch with your feelings will be very useful in not only understanding yourself better but strengthening your internal resilience. Below are words used to describe your emotions as you move through the exercises in this book. For those who struggle with understanding their feelings and putting language to them, it may be helpful to carry this feeling list around and use it as a reference. Consider circling the feelings you are experiencing in this moment.

Agitated	Appreciated	Chipper	Defensive
Alert	Ashamed	Comfortable	Dejected
Alienated	Astonished	Committed	Determined
Amazed	Awed	Concerned	Disappointed
Angry	Betrayed	Confident	Disdainful
Annoyed	Bitter	Confused	Disgusted
Anxious	Bored	Content	Eager
Apathetic	Calm	Curious	Embarrassed
Appalled	Caring	Dedicated	Encouraged

Energetic	Humiliated	Neglected	Scared
Enraged	Hurt	Nervous	Self-conscious
Enthusiastic	Inadequate	Numb	Serene
Envious	Independent	Offended	Shocked
Excited	Insecure	Optimistic	Silly
Fearful	Inspired	Ostracized	Stressed
Focused	Intrigued	Overwhelmed	Suspicious
Foolish	Irate	Peaceful	Tense
Fortunate	Irritated	Perplexed	Threatened
Frustrated	Jealous	Playful	Tired
Furious	Joyful	Powerful	Uncomfortable
Grateful	Lethargic	Productive	Uninterested
Grieving	Listless	Proud	Unworthy
Guilty	Lonely	Rejected	Vigilant
Happy	Lost	Relieved	Vulnerable
Honored	Loving	Resentful	Weak
Hopeful	Mad	Sad	Withdrawn
Hopeless	Miserable	Safe	Worried
Horrified	Motivated	Satisfied	

EXERCISE

While the above exercise aims to build awareness in the moment, the tracking exercise below helps to connect the feelings in your body to your thoughts and experiences. Identifying these three things—thoughts, feelings, and behaviors—will allow you to continue making resilient choices as you work through any crisis. Try completing the tracker below at least once a day. See if your responses and awareness of your body's feelings change over time. You may see more progress if you work to complete this tracker a few times a day. Try to complete the tracker in the morning, around midday, and at night.

	DAY 1	DAY 2	DAY 3	DAY 4	DAY 5
What feelings are you experiencing in this moment?					
Do you notice any thoughts arriving to your consciousness?					
What activated or triggered these thoughts?					
What does your body want to do with these thoughts/ feelings?					
Name one or two things you can do to cope with these thoughts/ feelings.					

Chapter 2

THE ROAD TO ADAPTATION

The only people who like change are babies in wet diapers.

—Herb Tannenbaum

Who doesn't have a love-hate relationship with change, right? Change is one of the great paradoxes of human existence—it can be difficult to move through, and it can result in some of the most incredible experiences in life. Change can be painful and terrifying at the moment—as with the loss of a loved one, the start of a new job, or the end of a relationship—but it can also bring you to newer, even better heights. During the global COVID-19 pandemic, most of the world was on "pause," but the world kept turning and people kept going. Relationships blossomed and ended, friends came and went, governments switched, and bodies became older and sicker. We deal with change all the time, and whether we are aware of it or not, we often adapt. Imagine waiting at an airport a few hours before boarding for a long-awaited vacation, then suddenly learning that the flight is canceled or delayed. Sure, a sudden change like that is irritating or, worse, infuriating; however, we ultimately realize that we need to stop fighting with reality and let go of feelings of bitterness that keep us stuck in a cycle of suffering. That said, we eventually must radically accept things that are out of our control to move on. Radical acceptance—a concept rooted in Buddhism and dialectical behavioral therapy (DBT) whereby you actively decide to detach from things you can't control—is key to overcoming your suffering.

Adaptability is a trait and a skill we need to survive and succeed. While adaptability is more difficult for some than others, it is inherent in each of us. For those who find it more challenging to move on from something, the goal is to build upon that intrinsic adaptability. You might ask yourself, if we all have this inherent adaptability, why does it feel so hard? Remember that humans are creatures of habit. We like predictability, and when faced with something new, we are often limited to two choices: do nothing or do something—and the "doing" something requires work. In the airport scenario when you learned that the fight was canceled, you would have had two choices: 1.) Do nothing and accept that you were not making the same flight, or 2.) Scramble and look for other flights out. While this example is trite, you get my point—adaptability takes work.

NEUROBIOLOGY AND THE BIOLOGY OF CHANGE

It may seem difficult at first, but everything is difficult at first.

—Miyamoto Musashi

Neuroplasticity is a key component of change. Neuroplasticity is the concept that the brain is malleable, and the ways our neurons are connected and fire off can adjust or change over time. There are two types of neuroplasticity: functional plasticity and structural plasticity. Functional plasticity is the brain's ability to move functions from a damaged area of the brain to undamaged areas. Take, for instance, a stroke victim relearning how to walk, talk, and use parts of their body impacted by the stroke. Structural plasticity is the brain's ability to change its physical structure because of learning, such as when we learn to play a sport or speak a new language.

At birth, every neuron in the cerebral cortex has approximately 2,500 synapses that relay neurotransmitters. When we reach three years old, we have about 15,000 synapses per neuron. By the time we are adults, we have about half of the number of synapses per neuron than we did when we were children. This results from a process called synaptic pruning, which allows some synapses to strengthen and others to diminish depending upon our experiences.[19] Essentially, by developing new connections, the brain can adapt to the changing environment.

EXERCISE

If the concept of neuroplasticity is new to you, it can be confusing, especially if you are prone to obsessive thinking about an idea or situation. In that case, you might be dubious about whether anything can change, especially if you have worked hard in the past to distract or "turn off" your thoughts. It can be challenging, but turning the off button takes work. Try this simple exercise and see what happens.

Step 1: Find a blank piece of paper and a pencil. Write your name on the top of the page.

Step 2: Notice the hand you used to write. Was it your left or right hand? Most people will notice that they wrote their names with their dominant hand.

Step 3: Put the pencil down and shake out your hands. Start writing your name on the paper with the opposite hand.

Step 4: What happened when you tried to write with your opposite hand? How did it feel to hold the pencil in your nondominant hand?

19 Alison Gopnik, Patricia K. Kuhl, and Andrew Meltzoff, *The Scientist in the Crib: Minds, Brains, and How Children Learn* (New York: Morrow, 2001), pp. 174–197.

Step 5: Repeat writing your name in your nondominant hand until you reach the end of the page. When you reach the end of the page, turn it over and do the same thing—write your name with your nondominant hand again and again.

Step 6: Notice how it feels. What do you imagine it would feel like if you were to do the same thing again in one minute—write your name with your nondominant hand?

Sure, this task is challenging. We all know that for most of us our brains are hardwired to have a dominant hand preference. However, despite its difficulty, you can train your brain to have a nondominant hand preference over time. You might have noticed that even with this exercise, writing with your nondominant hand was hard, *and* you could do it. My grandmother used to remind me that even though she was born left-handed, after 12 years of Catholic school and pressure from the nuns to write with her right hand, she was ambidextrous.

The point of this exercise is to demonstrate that even though your brain wants to do the easier, more efficient thing (i.e., write with your dominant hand) and unconsciously tells you that it is too hard or wrong to switch hands, you can. It makes sense for your brain to stop you when you do something radically different; however, over time and with practice, it gets easier to form new habits, new neurological pathways, and new skills. The take-home message is that you have a choice and the power to change and push through difficult things.

Consider what happens to our neurobiology when we partner and then break up with someone. During the beginning stages of love, a large part of why it feels so good is that there are regions in the brain that are rich in dopamine—a neurotransmitter that plays a key role in feeling pleasure. As a result, certain parts of the brain light up, and those parts of the brain that control fear and social judgment are operating at lower rates.[20]

In 2005, biological anthropologist and researcher Helen Fisher published a seminal study depicting the first functional MRI images of those in the beginning stages of love and those going through a breakup.[21] They learned that there was a change in brain chemistry. The MRIs of those who experienced unwanted breakups appeared to have similar brain scans to those who experienced withdrawal from addictive substances. In 2011, Edward Smith, director of cognitive neuroscience at Columbia University, studied individuals who felt intensely rejected after a breakup.[22] These individuals were asked to look at photos of their friends and think positive thoughts, as well as pictures of their exes while thinking about the breakup. In the resulting brain scans, areas of the brain related to external exposure to pain

---

20 Helen Fisher, "The Brain in Love," TED Talk, accessed March 28, 2023, https://www.ted.com/talks/helen_fisher_the_brain_in_love.

21 Helen E. Fisher et al., "Intense, Passionate, Romantic Love: A Natural Addiction? How the Fields That Investigate Romance and Substance Abuse Can Inform Each Other," *Frontiers in Psychology* 7 (May 10, 2016), https://doi.org/10.3389/fpsyg.2016.00687.

22 "Love Study: Brain Reacts to Heartbreak Same as Physical Pain," *Medical News Today* (MediLexicon International), accessed April 3, 2023, https://www.medicalnewstoday.com/articles/220427#1.

became active when the participants reflected on their exes. In summary, Smith's research posits that breakups can cause physical pain—making it much more challenging to adapt to the loss of a loved one, especially a romantic other.

The upside here is if this is your situation or if you have been in this situation, elements of neuroscience can be clutch in helping you heal from a breakup. While some of these recommendations may seem obvious, ways to best adapt to a recent heartbreak and rewire new neurologic connections include:

- Avoiding visual reminders of your ex that include pictures and places where you would spend time. Revisiting these images may create dopamine surges that may result in feelings of withdrawal once the stimuli are removed. This may be quite painful.

  » **Try:** Coming up with a list of alternative places to go instead of the places you frequented with your ex.

- Swapping the dopamine boost for an endorphin boost by working out.

  » **Try:** Joining a workout class or finding an accountability partner.

- Creating a list of the reasons why you are better off without your ex. List all of the toxic or unhealthy features of your relationship. Review this list whenever a positive thought crosses your mind.

  » **Try:** Keeping this list handy—maybe in your backpack, pocket, etc. Have it available so that if a thought about your ex crosses your mind, you can take a peek at the list. Other places to keep the list include a bedside table or on a sticky note by your computer.

- Doing meditation and mindfulness techniques.

  » **Try:** Breakup apps like Mend, Break-Up Boss, or Rx Breakup.

- Staying out of contact with your ex.

  » **Try:** Every time you have an urge or an impulse to contact your ex, try texting a friend or writing an email to yourself. Whatever you do, resist the temptation to contact them directly.

EXERCISE

Keeping the concept of neuroscience in mind, name the change(s) you are explicitly working on to overcome and identify how you feel about those changes.

I feel _____ about

_____(name the change).

I want to feel _____ about

_____(name the change).

THE *resilience* WORKBOOK FOR WOMEN

For this exercise, consider the current obstacle(s) that you are working to overcome while using the TIC-TOC technique. Rooted in cognitive behavioral therapy (CBT), the TIC-TOC technique can help people think more adaptively. This method, created by psychiatrist and author David Burns, helps people think more constructively by changing unhelpful thoughts that can fuel negative feelings and behaviors. Typically used to help people counter thoughts that contribute to procrastination, this technique can also be helpful to target mental barriers such as overcoming an ex or managing feelings around loss. The TIC stands for **T**ask-**I**nterfering **C**ognitions, and the TOC stands for **T**ask-**O**riented **C**ognitions. Essentially, the method asks for you to take stock of your thoughts, especially those negative thoughts or your TICS, so that you can swap in more helpful thoughts, your TOCS, that fuel your motivation. Look at an example of the TIC-TOC chart below. See if you can make your own chart. Take note of what you feel when you reframe your TICs into TOCs.

TICS (TASK-INTERFERING COGNITIONS)	TOCS (TASK-ORIENTED COGNITIONS)
Widow's **TIC**: I will never be able to move my husband's articles of clothing from our closet. It will be too hard.	**Swap this TIC for TOC. This is overgeneralized thinking.** Just do a little bit. You don't have to get rid of everything.
Woman going through fertility treatment's **TIC:** I have completed three rounds of IVF. It is never going to work.	**Swap this TIC for TOC. This is all-or-nothing thinking.** It may take a few more rounds. If you really want a child, there may be other options.
Menopausal woman's **TIC:** I am losing my looks and my youth. When I look at myself, I don't feel attractive.	**Swap this TIC for TOC. This is disqualifying the positive.** Even though you may be aging, there are many positive and attractive parts to you. Come up with your own list of reframes.
Name your TIC here:	Name your TOC here:
Name your TIC here:	Name your TOC here:

CHANGE MAKES US ALL A LITTLE NUTS

Working toward change is hard and can drive some of us NUTs—especially if you are like me and tend to ruminate. In fact, for some who ruminate, their constant negative thoughts can result in adverse bodily sensations. Ruminating or getting can stuck in a negative loop can result in anxious and depressive symptoms. For example, after a loved one's death, especially when it is sudden and unexpected, it is not uncommon to experience grief reactions such as problems sleeping, a change in appetite, and irritability, to name a few.

For some, adapting to the loss of a loved one if they pass can be excruciating. While most will move through the grief and pain and return to their routine within weeks or months of the event, this is not true for everyone. Some experience something called complicated grief, where they have trouble recovering from their loss and are unable to resume their typical life. Consider the case of Alison.

CASE SCENARIO

Alison, a 20-year-old student at NYU, came into my office after the traumatic loss of her mother. A year or so before starting therapy, Alison received a call from her father telling her that her mother had instantly died after a head-on collision on her way to work one morning. Alison was so traumatized by this loss that she decided to take a leave of absence from her undergraduate program and return home to take care of her father and younger brother. Alison and her family mourned. The family, who was of Jewish faith, sat shiva—a religious ritual where the family and friends of the deceased come together to heal spiritually and emotionally. A year later, Alison participated in the family's unveiling of her mother's tombstone. To Alison, it seemed as though both her father and brother had healed and moved on from her mother's passing. This fact deeply hurt Alison, who nearly a year and a half later was struggling to return to her undergraduate program. Each week Alison would come into therapy sharing how shocking the loss was and how challenging it was for her to not be able to call her mother or go home to see her mother. The loss of her mother changed her whole identity. Alison was very much stuck in the past and, as a result, was not able to create a new life or identity for herself. It was clear that the prolonged grief that Alison was experiencing impacted how she saw herself. Prior to her mother's passing, she described herself as a carefree, fun-loving, spirited young woman; but she had transformed into a person who was, as others described her, "walled off" and very sensitive. Such a drastic personality shift had implications for Alison's schooling and her personal life.

To reclaim the person that she was prior to the loss of her mother, Alison worked in large part to get out of the negative feedback loop that existed between her thoughts, feelings, and behaviors. If you are suffering from a loss like Alison's or from another difficult change, it is likely because of those automatic negative unconscious thoughts that pop up.

THE *resilience* WORKBOOK FOR WOMEN

Such negative unconscious thoughts, or NUTs thoughts as termed by psychologist Dr. Elisha Goldstein,[23] live beneath our awareness and include deep-rooted beliefs. It is no surprise that such negative unconscious thoughts elicit negative feelings such as depression and can hinder the ability to move forward with change ,on a psychological, emotional, and behavioral level.

Consider the impact that thinking, "Without my mom, I can't exist," could have on your feelings and behaviors. Imagine what could (and later did) happen if Alison could change this initial NUT into something more positive.

Eventually, Alison was able to reframe her initial NUT to something more positive—"My love for my mom will remain strong and I will survive." Surely, a much more positive automatic thought, which led to more positive feelings and the eventual reengagement of Alison with school and her social life as a more positive, bubbly person.

EXERCISE

Healing also means taking an honest look at the role you play in your own suffering.

—Smart Anonymous Person

By naming your NUTs, you not only bring awareness to them, but also take the first step in kicking them to the curb. It is an important skill to name your negative unconscious thoughts and counter and reframe them to be more positive. In the section below, examine the cognitive feedback loop.

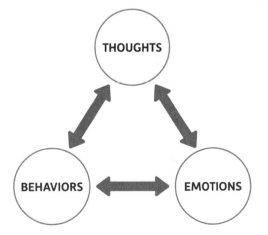

In the section below, name those negative unconscious thoughts getting in the way of your making progress toward change. Then, in the next column, identify a reframe or devise an alternative to that automatic negative thought.

23 Elisha Goldstein, *Uncovering Happiness: Overcoming Depression with Mindfulness and Self-Compassion* (United Kingdom: Simon and Schuster, 2015).

NAME YOUR NEGATIVE THOUGHTS	REFRAME THOSE NEGATIVE THOUGHTS

Humans tend to focus on the negative instead of the positive. If you are like me, you sometimes find yourself in a rut, ruminating on negative thoughts and not feeling so great.

This tendency, also known as negativity bias, makes sense, as our brains are wired to keep us safe from threats. As we evolved, our brains likely learned to see negative things as dangerous or threatening in order to protect us. Consider how you might react to receiving negative feedback from a manager. If you are anything like me, worrying that you may get fired or not get a bonus (for example) might cause a pit in your stomach, spiraling thoughts, and stress sweat. You get my point.

While naming the NUTs and cracking them are helpful, specific NUTs can be harder to break than others. Identifying the type of negative thinking you are experiencing may be beneficial when it is tough to crack your NUTs.

Consider the case of Shanequa.

CASE SCENARIO

Shanequa was 36 years old when her spouse of 16 years came home one day after visiting family for Easter and told her that he loved her but wasn't *in* love with her anymore. This news shocked Shanequa, who stewed and contemplated: *What did that mean?* Unfortunately, her husband didn't quite know what it meant, either. This statement surprised Shanequa, as she thought they had a peaceful, happy relationship.

Weeks and months went by without clarification. Understandably, Shanequa was anxious, with fearful thoughts. She questioned herself constantly. *Am I good enough? What did I do wrong? Am I too old? Why am I such a loser?* She also tended to return to the more challenging times in her relationship while discounting the many positive experiences. Suddenly, from Shanequa's perspective, all the good parts of her relationship were null and void.

In short, Shanequa's mind participated in a few types of negative thinking that led to unhealthy cognitive distortions. See more on the different types of negative thinking below.

EXERCISE

Don't be pushed around by the fears in your mind. Be led by the dreams in your heart.

—Roy T. Bennett

Review the categories of negative thinking that typically lead to negative distortions. Can you identify the types of negative thinking Shanequa experienced?

Identify the type of negative thinking you tend to do so you can kick it to the curb when it comes up. Consider the list below and circle the top two or three that resonate with you.

Polarization or dichotomous thinking: Essentially, having an all-or-nothing mindset, oversimplifying complex issues so that there is no middle ground or room for compromise (i.e., things are black and white or good or bad).[24]

Emotional reasoning: Insisting that something is true even though the only evidence is based on feelings. Someone engaging in emotional reasoning leans into negative emotions and creates a narrative to justify their feelings. "I feel anxious about driving to work today, so something dangerous or bad will happen at work."

Overgeneralization: The tendency to fixate on one negative detail or experience and overblow its significance in your life. For example, getting the slightest negative feedback from a supervisor then

---

24 "Cognitive Distortions Explained with 10 Examples," UPMC Healthbeat, accessed March 28, 2023, https://share.upmc.com/2021/05/cognitive-distortions.

automatically assuming you are the worst employee and will get fired. The despairing notion is not proportionate to the event that triggered it.

Labeling: Putting negative labels on yourself and the things around you. A more extreme version of all-or-nothing feeling (see "polarization or dichotomous thinking" on page 39). If something negative happens, you might label yourself as "a fool" or "a failure" or "stupid." Labeling is quite irrational and causes someone to assume that they are their behavior. Those who label may also see others similarly. This could happen when someone around you engages in negative behavior, and as a result, you label that person. For instance, when someone cuts you off, you may call them a jerk, even though you have no idea if that is true. The only truth is that they engaged in the negative behavior of cutting you off.

"Should have, would have, could have" thinking: Telling yourself that things should be how you expect them to be. "Should" statements directed toward yourself can lead to guilt, frustration, and depression. For instance, "I should not have engaged in that fight—if I hadn't, maybe we would still be together."

Mental filtering: When faced with a difficult situation, you choose, consciously or unconsciously, to focus on only the bad part of the situation and dwell on it exclusively so that this colors the entire experience as being negative. Say you are giving a talk at work and even though it was received well by most listeners, you obsess about the one piece of feedback that was marginally critical and allow that to become how you see that experience.

Catastrophizing: Catastrophizing, also known as magnification, typically occurs in the heat of the moment. It looks like someone blowing an issue out of proportion. An example is letting a delay at an airport ruin your entire vacation.

Discounting the positive: Like mental filtering, discounting the positive is tending to reject most positive experiences in favor of insisting that the positive experiences don't count. If you do a good job at one thing, you may tell yourself that it wasn't good enough or that anyone else could have done as good of a job as you did. When you discount the positives of experiences, it takes the pleasure out and can leave you feeling depressed and unfulfilled.

Personalization and blaming: This pattern of behavior is when you hold yourself responsible for an event that is not at all or entirely in your control. Consider a trauma victim who told herself, "My trauma only happened because I was out late and had too many drinks." Personalization and blaming yourself, especially when it is out of your control, can put you at risk of guilt, shame, and inadequacy.

Although this list is not an exhaustive list of all the cognitive distortions that can lead to negative emotions, they top the list of the most frequently cited distortions.

Note the distorted ways of thinking that apply most to you. When you fall into these unhealthy patterns, consider being more intentional about your thinking process. For instance, imagine what could have been different for Shanequa if she slowed down and said to herself, "I think I am having a negative thought," versus leaning into the initial negative thought, which in turn may have resulted in more negative thoughts and even negative feelings.

What would it be like to catch yourself in the moment before you lean into cognitive distortions? How would this change how you feel? Would the cognitive distortion become less real? Try this the next time you notice that you are leaning into those negative thoughts.

EXERCISE

We suffer more often in imagination than in reality.

—Seneca

Considering the list of distorted ways of thinking, can you conceptualize what would be different if a thought was *just a fleeting thought*? Experts estimate that the mind has about 60,000 to 80,000 thoughts per day, which means we have approximately 3,000 thoughts per hour.[25] What would happen if, when you have a NUT or a cognitive distortion, you consider it *just one* thought among the sixty or eighty thousand you will likely have in the day?

Imagine that your NUTs or cognitive distortions are like stars on an exceptionally starry night. In this context, you can choose to focus on many different stars. In this image, you notice that most of the stars look alike and radiate the same amount of energy. In this guided imagery, ask yourself how you decide which stars to focus on and why.

Consider applying this mental exercise when you notice your negative thoughts.

Which thought are you focusing on?

....

Why is this the thought you are getting stuck on:

....

....

---

25 Neuroskeptic, "The 70,000 Thoughts Per Day Myth?" *Discover Magazine*, May 9, 2012.

In the universe of all of thoughts, what are some other thoughts that you might not have access to you because you are focusing your attention on this one thought? Write down as many of those other thoughts as you can here:

_____

_____

_____

_____

_____

_____

_____

_____

What if you considered NUTs or cognitive distortions as shooting stars? You quickly catch a glimpse of them as they dart across the night sky, and then poof, they're gone.

EXERCISE

Your attitude is like a box of crayons that color your world. Constantly color your picture gray, and your picture will always be bleak. Try adding some bright colors to the picture by including humor, and your picture begins to lighten up.

—Allen Klein

When working through a challenging change, it can be hard to think clearly, especially if the change has the potential to be life-altering. Just as with the saying, "seeing things through rose-colored glasses," where you tend to see only the good points in a situation, sometimes, in periods of difficulty, we tend to see no positives, essentially seeing things with "dark-colored sunglasses."

For this exercise, compare how you see something with your dark-colored sunglasses on versus off. Below each pair of glasses, describe what might be different. For instance, typically when one is wearing dark shades, the colors and the vibrancy of life around them may be a bit subdued as compared to when one may be wearing their clear, prescription glasses and seeing all the vibrancy (for better or worse) that life has to offer.

Imagine you are wearing your dark-colored glasses. Write down what you see.

....

....

....

Now, metaphorically speaking, put on your regular, clear-colored glasses. If you were to look at the same situation while wearing these glasses, write down what you would see.

....

....

....

Remember: You have the power and the choice about when to put on and take off each pair of glasses. In the future you may want to ask yourself which pair of glasses with which you'd want to view your current situation.

EXERCISE

Rewiring the brain takes time and a lot of work. At the same time, processing feelings is an integral part of the healing process. That said, it is essential to create time and a safe place to sit through the discomfort and all the feelings that change brings. Containing your pain while adjusting can be helpful as you move through your journey. Remember that if feelings remain unprocessed, there is the risk that you will tuck them away, only for them to bubble back up in the future.

Some helpful strategies that help create space while simultaneously containing your feelings include:

Creating a specific amount of time each day to sit, journal, or reflect on the change that is before you. Set a timer for 10 to 15 minutes a day; when your time is up, it is up. Know that you can return to these negative thoughts and feelings tomorrow. Over time, try to decrease the time allocated to this exercise.

Throughout the week, whenever you have negative thoughts or feelings, write them down on a small piece of paper, fold them, and put them into a jar. Once these negative thoughts and feelings are stored in the jar, allocate time weekly to review them. Again, set aside a specific amount of time—a maximum 30 minutes each week—to review your written thoughts and feelings. Open each piece of paper and reflect on that thought or feeling. Intentionally ask yourself, "Do I need this thought or feeling anymore?" If so, which parts do I need? If you no longer need a thought or feeling, rip up the entire piece of paper and trash it. If you need a thought or a feeling, put it back in the jar for the next time. If you only need a part of that thought or feeling, tear the paper proportionally to what you want to get rid of and toss that while leaving the remainder of the paper in the jar.

Chapter 3

AUTHORING YOUR NARRATIVE

You are the author of your own life story. You have the leading role and get to
determine how you interact with your supporting cast and other characters.
Without realizing it, you may have allowed the events in your life to write your story
for you rather than taking deliberate action to write it in your own voice. What
will it take to love your life story to create the happy endings you desire?

—Susan C. Young

Humans are story writers. We like to tell stories and have them come alive. Consider newly pregnant parents who chatter about their unborn child, dreaming and fantasizing about their baby's future. *Will it be a boy or a girl? Will the child follow in their mother's footsteps and play soccer? Our child will never eat fast food. When they grow up, they will go to our alma mater. Our child will help take care of us when we are older.*

There it is: when we are born, we are placed in a set (our homes) with a cast of characters (our caretakers) who have expectations and perceptions. As a result, at some point, we each internalize such expectations and perceptions, and as the saying goes, perception is our reality.

As a result, many of us walk around with a little script inside our heads of what we should be doing. The script helps us confirm how we are "performing" relative to our expectations and perceptions of ourselves. For instance, if the script says, "Make law partner by age 36 years old," and we do, then the script and reality align. Check! We write that off as a win. If the script says, "get married by 25, buy a house, get a dog, and have two kids before 35," and we do—check! Another win. If you look closely, there is a pattern in such scripts. The narratives we develop early in life can often lead us into very narrow, inflexible ways of thinking. For instance, "If I can't complete this (name whatever your internal script or narrative is of yourself), then I must be a failure." An unfortunate consequence of internalized, inflexible narratives.

The above statement might seem harsh on an intellectual level, so why not have some self-compassion? Easier said than done, especially since our internal narratives/scripts are often how we see ourselves and how we represent ourselves to the world. As stories often do, our narratives have emotions and meanings, and each of our stories helps us make meaning of who, why, and where we are at any given time.

But what happens when life, as it often does, goes off script? Instead of making law partner by age 36, you receive a cancer diagnosis, take medical leave and out of necessity forgo the next step to being a law-firm partner. Or you get married by age 25 but learn that you are infertile, and even after the four rounds of IVF, there is no pregnancy.

When our lives go off script, it can be terrifying and ungrounding. For some, going "off-script" can undermine generational narratives. Consider the case of the law assistant about to make partner. Perhaps her narrative is built upon her grandparent's migration story and her parents' narrative of working round the clock as store clerks at a corner store to pay for her college and law school. Our narratives sometimes are not just ours—they may be that of our ancestors. Understandably, changes to our narrative, especially when we get locked into a particular way of viewing things, can be hugely destabilizing and, for some, can result in diagnosable anxiety, stress, and depression.

A primary conduit for resilience is your ability to choose or transform your current narrative in the face of adversity.[26] While we may not have the power or the resources to change the adverse event, we each have the ability and the choice to view them in entirely different ways, as Lucy and Jackie do in the case scenario below.

CASE SCENARIO

May we trust in the unfolding and meet it well.

—Pslam 37:3

Lucy and Jackie were two women in their late thirties. Lucy had been trying to conceive a child just before learning about her partner's infidelity. Lucy started therapy with the mindset of "Why did this happen to me? This is the worst news of my life. My life is *over*."

Jackie had also been trying to conceive when she found out her partner was unfaithful. While profoundly hurt by her partner's affair, she held on to a sense of optimism. Jackie broke up with her partner and moved on.

On the other hand, Lucy had difficulty moving on after she and her partner separated. She was devastated and held onto the fixed, negative narrative. Lucy struggled for a while and remained locked in the assumption that her ex was her "forever." She could not conceptualize moving on and dating other men. One day, while walking her dog, she saw her ex-partner out on a date. This finally motivated her to start dating again. After a few online dates, Lucy was

26 Caroline Lenette, Mark Brough, and Leonie Cox, "Everyday Resilience: Narratives of Single Refugee Women with Children," *Qualitative Social Work* 12, no. 5 (June 11, 2012): pp. 637–653, https://doi.org/10.1177/1473325012449684.

smitten. Before this experience, Lucy never would have envisioned herself falling for another person. Had she remained stuck in this mindset, Lucy would not have had the opportunity to find romance again. Both Lucy and Jackie found romance and healthier new partnerships.

As these case scenarios illuminate, approaching life from a fixed mindset can leave us feeling stuck, hopeless, and depressed. Sometimes, we can get so caught up in these negative thoughts that they taint even the positives we experience.

I can relate to this experience firsthand. I had a painful experience with my long-term partner a few years ago. He was suffering emotionally and working through a midlife crisis. We decided to take a break. Eventually, this short-term break became permanent. There was nothing more painful than this decision. Of course, in the moment, I couldn't see any silver lining—I would have to move from the apartment I shared with my best friend and start over. At 37 years old, during the COVID shutdown I lived on my own for the first time since college. Truthfully, I was despondent. Never could I have ever portended that this would be my life. In my family of origin, such breakups didn't happen. I wondered what I had done wrong. I had envisioned having my practice, children, and a long life with this person I had been partnered with for over 16 years. As I moved on, I decided that I deserved someone who felt I was too important to lose and held on to my girlfriend's words: *Maybe he was your starter husband.* From the moment my friend said those words, I embraced that sentiment and decided to let the story of my old life pass away. I was now free to create a newer, more authentic narrative and take physical and emotional journeys that never would have been allowed had my former story continued. I went on adventures with new people, made new friends, met a new partner, am on good terms with my former partner, and now have the pleasure of an adolescent in my life—all things that I thought I had to give up when my old narrative died. The truth is that the old narrative didn't entirely die, it just became richer, enhanced by a brilliant story of resilience. Knowing my luck (good and bad), my story will likely continue to take many twists and turns, and even deepen if I keep an open and flexible mindset.

The truth is that there is nothing particularly unique to my narrative or Jackie's. So often, I hear stories like this when someone decides to lean into the unknown and let go of a set narrative. Many find it to be freeing. Being flexible and authoring your narrative is a gift you can give yourself, your future, and your past.

EXERCISE

Putting the pen (yes, an actual pen) to paper can help rewire your neurologic connections, especially if you need to strengthen some connections for change to occur. That said, there is value in writing down aspects of your current narrative and exploring the best-case scenarios that may happen once you endeavor to move forward with this change.

For this exercise, consider yourself a playwright. You are working with one script that can be enhanced and improved, and the new script may have a different middle and end.

To begin, think about your current narrative. Think about the beginning, middle, and end. Feel free to expand on this exercise outside of the workbook.

Beginning:

_____

_____

_____

_____

_____

_____

_____

_____

Middle:

_____

_____

_____

_____

_____

_____

_____

_____

_____

_____

End:

_____

_____

_____

_____

_____

_____

_____

Now think about what your narrative can be. Depending on where you are in your journey, you can change the beginning, middle, or end. Imagine what the alternatives can be. Write them down below. Feel free to expand on this exercise outside of the workbook.

Beginning:

_____

_____

_____

_____

_____

_____

_____

_____

Middle:

_____

_____

_____

_____

_____

_____

_____

_____

End:

_____

_____

_____

_____

_____

_____

_____

_____

_____

THE *resilience* WORKBOOK FOR WOMEN

GOODBYE, HELLO

A sense of loss often occurs in the shift from one narrative to another. Saying "goodbye" or "so long, for now" is the most challenging part of the process of rewriting your narrative. The kind of loss you experience can leave you searching for answers. For example, the loss you feel because of infertility, miscarriage, a breakup, losing a friendship, experiencing a natural disaster, or even a pandemic may not always result in closure—making it hard to move through feelings of sadness and depression.

This is opposed to the death of a loved one, where there is a more physical closure—a funeral, maybe an explanation of the cause of death, and a memorial service.

It is also important to note that secondary losses sometimes come with primary losses. Secondary losses occur because of the primary loss but don't emerge until weeks or months afterward. Often, secondary losses are unique to the change that occurred. Examples of secondary losses can be:

- Loss of income
- Loss of a home
- Loss of financial security
- Loss of a community
- Loss of relational identity (no longer a spouse, partner, friend)
- Loss of roles (e.g., being the primary caretaker, breadwinner, etc.)
- Loss of sense of self
- Loss of confidence
- Loss of hope for the future
- Loss of goals/dreams

Regardless of the loss, it is critical that we process our feelings around it and grieve appropriately so that we can, in earnest, move forward with re-authoring our new narrative.

Consider the case of Joon.

CASE SCENARIO

Joon, a first-generation Chinese American, had always envisioned her life with a partner, two kids, a cat, and a house in suburban New Jersey. In Joon's narrative, she would be an Ivy League school mother whose children excelled at academics and athletics. Joon had concocted this narrative at the ripe old age of 10 years old when she was playing school and house with her older sister. Joon's vision came together quickly. By age 27, she was the assistant principal at her school; by 30, she was married; and four years later, Joon had twins. About 10 years into her "dream" life in suburban New Jersey, one of her twin sons started to demonstrate dangerous behavior in his elementary school.

Joon and her partner were suddenly inundated with calls from concerned teachers at her son's school. Playdates stopped, and Joon's son spent most of his time in the principal's office.

One day the school had to call EMS to take Joon's son to the emergency room as his behavior escalated to the point of no control. After this event, Joon and her partner were overwhelmed by the series of psychiatric, individual therapy, and family counseling appointments that they and their son had to attend. He was sent to a psychiatric facility in upstate New York, where he was diagnosed with pediatric psychosis—a severe and chronic mental illness. One thing was clear, however: this was a significant detour in Joon's narrative for herself and her family.

Following her son's diagnosis and his experience of being in and out of hospitals, Joon experienced grief. Her son's condition drastically impacted her sense of self and the future she saw for her family. Could this son function and navigate the world to be a high performer at the caliber of the Ivy League? Would her son even be able to live alone as he transitioned into young adulthood? Joon had similar questions about her role as a mother—Was she good enough? Where did she go wrong? What could she have done differently?

Not only had Joon's longstanding narrative shifted, but the family's functioning was also impacted, from how the family organized daily activities of living to keep up with her son's appointments to their financial well-being (impacted by paying for mental health care, behavioral support, etc.) to her relationship with her husband and other son. Families were too afraid of his behavior, which resulted in fewer play dates and less socialization within the community overall. Joon and her husband had to take time off from work to provide their son with emotional support and to take him to and from even more appointments than before. Joon was no longer seen as the type A overachiever at work but as someone barely pulling her weight among her colleagues. Just as quickly as Joon's dream had come alive, it was taken away from her.

Joon and her family experienced the loss of their son and their lives as they knew them before his erratic behavior. This ambiguous loss was painful as it not only reconfigured their future narratives, but they had to grieve multiple losses—the dreams, the friends, their roles, financial stability, etc. Over time, Joon moved forward from this pain and, in her way, created a new meaning for herself and her family. Joon eventually became a parent advocate at the National Association of Mental Illness (NAMI.org), where she educated and supported other families going through similar struggles. Joon's participation in this program gave her a new sense of self-confidence, identity, meaning, and purpose.

EXERCISE

In the case of building resiliency around any loss, it is imperative to be able to identify the primary loss and the secondary loss. In the case of Joon, the primary loss was her son's mental health stability, and the secondary losses that followed consisted of community, financial stability, identity, etc.

Name the primary loss associated with your change at hand:

....

....

THE *resilience* WORKBOOK FOR WOMEN

Can you name the secondary losses, if applicable, related to the primary loss that this change provokes?

....

....

Can you identify the feelings/emotions/energy in your body as you think about these losses? If so, how are you feeling, and where in your body (head, shoulders, solar plexus, stomach, arms, legs, etc.) do you feel it?

....

....

....

....

Can you list the potential gains or upside to the primary or secondary losses?

....

....

....

....

MAKING MEANING OF YOUR NEW SITUATION

The research around grief has grown over the past decade. Historically, researchers and clinicians leaned into the famous Kubler-Ross model of grief,[27] which entails five linear stages: denial, anger, bargaining, depression, and acceptance.

More recent thinking suggests that moving through these stages of grief is not linear and that grief never goes away entirely; it just gets smaller.[28] In her book, *Resilient Grieving,* Lucy Hone, PhD, asserts

---

27 Waquar Siddiqui et al., "Kubler-Ross Stages of Dying and Subsequent Models of Grief," 2023, https://www.ncbi.nlm.nih.gov/books/NBK507885.

28 Patia Braithwaite, "What Happens When Your Grief Doesn't Go Away?," *SELF*, August 2, 2019, https://www.self.com/story/heres-when-its-time-to-see-someone-about-grief.

that those who have close family ties, community support, a positive attitude, the presence of role models, and an optimistic outlook on life are better at coping with loss.[29] Hone further asserts that managing grief varies for everyone and that those most successful at overcoming grief address their loss with intentionality and re-focus their attention on the present rather than the past. For many of us, the most challenging part of change is physically, mentally, and emotionally living in the present and holding hope for the future. Especially in ambiguous loss, when unanswered questions are abundant—What does this all mean? Will anything ever work out? What is my purpose? What is the meaning of life?

If we are lucky, we fall into an opportunity where creating a new narrative is easy, as with Joon's participation in NAMI, which gave her a new sense of purpose and identity—essentially enabling her to make meaning out of her son's challenges. With this new sense of meaning, it was easier for Joon to move through some of her son's mental and behavioral difficulties. Joon now had a new set of goals to accomplish—to help other parents who were experiencing similar challenges—which helped her feel more optimistic about her future.

Unfortunately, not all of us will be as lucky as Joon, to access something that can offer us meaning and catapult us into a new, fresh narrative. Instead, sometimes we must be more intentional and proactive about finding a purpose and new meaning from our experiences. Take the story of Holocaust survivor, author, psychiatrist, and philosopher Viktor Frankl. In his seminal work, *Man's Search for Meaning*, he shares his experiences in a Nazi concentration camp and how he decided to proactively find a sense of purpose amid the chaos of losing his wife to the violence.[30] Frankl decided to provide medical support to fellow prisoners who were sick with illness. Not only did caring for his comrades provide him with a sense of purpose and meaning; it also enabled him to transcend this adversity and, once the war was over, develop a new type of therapy called logotherapy, which helps people identify and generate a sense of purpose and meaning for themselves in the face of adversity. Perhaps, the most significant takeaway from Frankl's experience is twofold: 1.) No one can take away your attitude toward suffering or your ability to derive meaning from your adversity, and 2.) Two things that are diametric opposites of one another can be true simultaneously, essentially allowing the "Both/And" of a situation. In Frankl's narrative, he details the pain and suffering of himself and others while also fantasizing about the future and gaining pleasure in noticing the beauty of nature. Consider the case of Jennifer and her experience with Both/And.

CASE SCENARIO

Jennifer came to see me after she learned that she was struggling with secondary infertility—a woman's inability to conceive or carry a pregnancy to term after giving birth. Jennifer and her partner had been trying to conceive their second child for over two years when she came to see me to process her experiences and grief. When Jennifer started treatment, she

29 Lucy Hone and Karen Reivich, *Resilient Grieving: How to Find Your Way through a Devastating Loss* (New York, NY: The Experiment, 2017).

30 Viktor E. Frankl, Harold S. Kushner, and William J. Winslade, *Man's Search for Meaning* (Boston, MA: Beacon Press, 2006).

experienced four miscarriages and three failed IVF treatments. She and her partner had decided to take some time off from trying to reassess their next steps. Jennifer's partner was also concerned about the toll this loss was having on their marriage and her mental health.

Throughout treatment, Jennifer doubted her ability to move forward in the grieving process and would articulate her despondency about recovering from such experiences. At her lowest of lows, Jennifer doubted whether she would have the capacity to return to some place within herself where she was okay and to parent if she were to carry a pregnancy to term. If there was ever a time that Jennifer needed to summon her reserves of resilience, it was at this moment. Working through such negative thinking and feelings was difficult. Not only was there the presence of ambiguous loss (Jennifer's thought that there would never be another baby), but there was the present grief of the past pregnancies. The most formidable challenge for Jennifer was her ability to hold the Both/And of the situation.

Much of my work with Jennifer was not to replace her negative thoughts or feelings with happier cognitions or emotions but to help her hold space for two contradictory things simultaneously. This is known as dialectical thinking—essentially holding the "Both/And" of an experience.

Some of the themes I heard in our work together sounded something like this:

"I am never going to have another baby."

"My body is not working as it should."

"I have lost too many future children."

"This isn't fair; I have done everything right to provide a safe and healthy environment for this pregnancy."

"My husband does not understand my grief and he never will understand my pain."

The philosopher Hegel proposes that holding the "Both/And" contradictions at the same time are not problems but a way to help us move forward.[31] That said, we can't escape the reality that life is multidimensional and complicated and can't be explained in absolutes (e.g., good vs. bad; happy vs. sad).

EXERCISE

So how does one notice their absolute thinking and get comfortable with dialectical thinking? The first thing to do is to look at your all-or-nothing thinking or any extreme thinking (e.g., *I will never be happy again).* Take note of it in the spaces below.

---

31 David Cloud, "Hegelian Dialectics: The Devil's Winning Tool," Hegelian Dialectics: The Devil's Winning Tool, April 23, 2008, https://www.wayoflife.org/database/hegelian_dialectics_devils_winning_tool.html.

1. _____

2. _____

3. _____

4. _____

5. _____

Now, think about what it would look like to take any of these thoughts and consider if something contradictory can also be true, creating the Both/And.

See examples of how Jennifer was later able to utilize dialectical thinking.

ALL-OR-NOTHING THINKING	DIALECTICAL THINKING
"I am never going to have another baby."	I may not have another baby the way I imagined, and I may have another child in my life in another way.
"My body is not working as it should."	My body does the best given the circumstances, and I need to have more compassion for what it has done for me in the past and its future capacity.
"I have lost too many future children."	I will always grieve my pregnancy losses, and I do not know what my future has in store for me.
"This isn't fair; I have done everything right to provide a safe and healthy environment for this pregnancy."	I am devastated by what I have lost, and I am grateful for what I have.
"My husband does not understand my grief, and he never will understand my pain."	While my husband may not understand my experience of grief, I can share with him more about how my pain interferes with the way I function on a daily basis.

Now, take your thoughts, try to utilize dialectical thinking, and see if you can see the "Both/And" of the situation. Notice that when we can hold both thoughts, more flexibility and space often emerge.

1. _____

2. _____

3. _____

4. _____

5. _____

THE *resilience* WORKBOOK FOR WOMEN

Ask yourself how it feels to hold your initial thoughts along with a contradictory thought. Can you imagine reminding yourself of these truths as you move forward?

ACCEPTING THE NEW YOU AND YOUR FUTURE SELF

As grief theory posits, the last and final stage of grief is acceptance. While new bereavement research suggests that grief never goes away (it just gets smaller), acceptance is a primary key to moving forward from a loss or with a new change. For instance, when a loved one dies, as hard as it might be, we eventually come to terms with the new fact—that nothing will ever bring them back, no matter what we do or how hard we try. Most of us engage in a closing ceremony—a shiva, a funeral, a burial, or a memorial service—and when we leave that ceremony, we embark on our new life. Obviously, how easy or difficult this process is depends on the individual. However, the likely reality is that closure and moving forward are more challenging when there is an unclear or ambiguous loss. Sure, you can work to hold two things to be true, as evidenced in the case of Jennifer, but say in her situation, there are no more pregnancies. You may be thinking, how does one get over that?

The push-pull between holding onto hope and letting go can be the most painful part of any change-related experience. It is also important to note that much suffering results from our attachment to that pain. A fundamental principle in Buddhism is that attaching to people, material things, and specific outcomes causes suffering, as the only constant in the universe is change and, with change, there always is a loss. When you become attached to something, someone, or a specific narrative, you are more likely to experience suffering. Staying in a state of despair prevents you from moving forward and may result in a state of being perpetually stuck.

What does this mean, exactly? For starters, radical acceptance can be freeing. Most of us would be surprised by how often we radically accept things daily. Consider when you are running a few minutes late to a meeting due to traffic or if you are stuck underground on a subway. In such situations, you can't control the outcome—sure, you can choose to get angry, but having those feelings will not change the issue. So eventually, you accept that you are stuck in traffic or underground in a subway. Notice that radical acceptance does not involve the approval of the situation; instead, it consists of accepting the reality of the problem and not getting caught up in the emotional reaction.

EXERCISE

A core component of radical acceptance is watching your thoughts and feelings to identify when you are allowing yourself to feel worse than you need to. How will I know if I am, in general, a radically accepting person or need work in this area? For this exercise, it may be helpful to think about something you are struggling to accept and that seems impossible to move forward from.

Name your current challenge: _____

_____

For the following thoughts, feelings, or behaviors, circle yes or no depending on whether the statement resonates with you when thinking about your particular struggle.

STATEMENT	YES	NO
1. This isn't fair.	1	0
2. This is a learning opportunity.	0	1
3. Why is this happening to me?	1	0
4. Even if I cannot overcome this obstacle, I will be okay.	0	1
5. The situation that I am in right now is not okay.	1	0
6. I will never be okay with the situation before me.	1	0
7. I worry that I will not be able to overcome this.	1	0
8. The universe only puts things in front of you that you can manage.	0	1
9. You feel optimistic about what lies ahead for you.	0	1
10. I feel like I can never get a break.	1	0
11. I feel hopeless about moving past this situation.	1	0
12. I take good care of myself (i.e., eating healthy, working out, meditation, good sleep hygiene).	0	1
13. I feel broken on the inside.	1	0
14. To be heard and get any help around this situation, I need to nag others.	1	0
15. It is hard for me to get over what has happened in the past.	1	0
16. It is easy for me to let go and forgive others.	0	1
17. Everything seems to always work out.	0	1
18. What doesn't break you makes you stronger.	0	1

STATEMENT	YES	NO
19. I feel that with the right guidance, I am confident that I can overcome all odds.	0	1
20. You cannot change another's behaviors, just your own to move forward.	0	1
My Score		

Now, add up the 0s and 1s.

If your total is 8 or more, it may be indicative that you may need more practice in radical acceptance. If your total is between 4 and 7, you may be on your way to radically accepting the challenge before you but are not yet there.

If your total is between 0 and 3, you may be finding it easier to move forward from your challenge.

EXERCISE

This exercise will help you practice implementing radical acceptance. Below, identify three things that need radical acceptance. Choose three things that vary in difficulty of acceptance (i.e., ranging between easy, moderate, and difficult). Write them down below.

Easy: ....

Medium: ....

Difficult: ....

Find a comfortable place to sit. Either close your eyes or focus your vision on a spot in your space. First, clench all your muscles tight for approximately 10 seconds or so. Then release. Take an inventory of how your body feels now.

You will try this exercise again, but now you will think about the easiest thing you can accept.

Get comfortable and clench your muscles again, this time for 25 seconds. Then release. Upon this release, imagine radically accepting whatever is before you. Take an inventory of how your body feels now.

....

....

....

....

Do the same exercise again but consider something that is moderately difficult for you to accept. This time clench your muscles for 50 seconds. Then release. Upon this release, imagine radically accepting whatever is before you. Take an inventory of how your body feels now.

_____

_____

_____

Try doing the same thing with something difficult for you to accept. Clench your muscles again for 90 seconds. Then release. Upon this release, imagine radically accepting whatever is before you. Take an inventory of how your body feels now.

_____

_____

_____

Remember that radical acceptance is a choice that you must make with intentionality. This exercise aims to explore how it feels to accept something of varying degrees of difficulty radically and for your body to notice how it feels.

If your score indicated that you need some further support in developing your capacity for radical acceptance, you may want to consider the following **R.A.D.I.C.A.L.** strategies.

Realize what is happening around you when you struggle to accept a hard truth. Notice when you are questioning your current circumstances or fighting the truth of your situation.

Acknowledge the feelings that arise within your body when reminded of your challenge. Notice the feelings of discomfort. Just acknowledge that they are present and do your best to not lean into them.

Decide to focus on the positive outcomes that will result from you accepting the difficult challenge before you. Write down the reasons why moving past this challenge is beneficial for you in the long run.

Introspection is a fundamental part of radical acceptance and allows for one to examine and learn from one's past and move forward with greater ease. The practice of introspection starts with asking yourself questions about the current situation and what in your past brought you to where you are on now on your journey. You may consider asking yourself about what was really going on when you made certain choices for yourself.

Compassion is another core component of radical acceptance. Maintaining a stance of compassion for yourself and perhaps what you learned about yourself when reflecting on your choices and your current pain is important. We are all humans—meaning that we all have likely experienced similar feelings to varying degrees at one point or another. Additionally, compassion can be hugely helpful when trying to accept something that is difficult. Could you consider having empathy for others who may be involved in the challenge you are working to accept—e.g., the ex-partner with whom you just broke up with or your boss who had to have the difficult conversation of letting you go from your job?

Align yourself so that you are living a life that is congruent with your values and the person you want to grow into after you have moved beyond this challenge. One tip for alignment is spending time with people with whom you can be your best self and that share similar values and lifestyle practices.

Love yourself and others. Tremendous empowerment can come from loving oneself and others, and learning how to love all parts of someone (and yourself)—the good, the bad, and the ugly parts—is often the greatest barrier to radical acceptance. However, we often forget that loving yourself and others is a choice.

EXERCISE

Considering the R.A.D.I.C.A.L acronym above, can you consider a current challenge that is particularly difficult to overcome and assess what parts of radical acceptance you need to spend more time on?

Name your current challenge: ....

....

Name what you are realizing about the current challenge.

....

....

....

....

Acknowledge and list all the feelings that arise within your body when you are reminded of your challenge.

....

....

....

....

CHEERS TO NEW FUTURES

Meaning and purpose are essential to our survival; without these two core tenets, why would anyone get up in the morning? If you are reading this book, you may be at a crossroads to finding a new meaning and purpose to catapult you into your next chapter—your future. Researchers from the University of Michigan published a report that discussed how having a sense of purpose helped increase the longevity of those 50 years old and older.[32] Additional longitudinal research conducted by the Harvard Growing Up Today Study (GUTS) found that young adults with a clear sense of purpose evidenced in their day-to-day activities were happier and reported more positive physical and mental health outcomes.[33] This becomes even clearer when we look at how Viktor Frankl found purpose and a sense of meaning as a helper while imprisoned in the Nazi concentration camps. When moving forward in your new narrative, it is essential to understand the nuanced difference between purpose and meaning. Purpose is defined as "aspirations that motivate our activities,"[34] whereas meaning refers to "how we make sense of our life and roles in it.[35] For many, having a purpose and meaning are mutually exclusive; without them, our lives lack a story.

While Frankl proposed that the meaning of life can be discovered in three ways—creating work or accomplishing a task, experiencing something fully or loving somebody, and choosing your attitude toward suffering—other researchers and philosophers have expanded on this concept. Perhaps the most prominent framework comes from the work of researchers who put forth that when taken together, meaning is having a sense of purpose, coherence, and significance in the world.[36] In this context, an example of coherence is adapting and creating patterns that allow you to have a heightened sense of efficacy. A good example of coherence is building a routine to work toward a goal, such as going to the gym regularly to build strength and endurance. The third dimension, significance, focuses on the inherent value and work of one's life. For instance, your choice to invest your time in something worthwhile, say spending quality time with your family versus aimlessly watching television.

32 Aliya Alimujiang et al., "Association between Life Purpose and Mortality among US Adults Older than 50 Years," *JAMA Network Open* 2, no. 5 (May 24, 2019), https://doi.org/10.1001/jamanetworkopen.2019.4270.

33 Chen et al., "Sense of Mission and Subsequent Health and Well-Being among Young Adults: An Outcome-Wide Analysis," *American Journal of Epidemiology* 188, no. 4 (January 12, 2019): pp. 664–673, https://doi.org/10.1093/aje/kwz009.

34 Robert A. Emmons, "Personal Goals, Life Meaning, and Virtue: Wellsprings of a Positive Life.," *Flourishing: Positive Psychology and the Life Well-Lived.*, n.d., pp. 105-128, https://doi.org/10.1037/10594-005.

35 Itai Ivtzan et al., *Second Wave Positive Psychology: Embracing the Dark Side of Life* (London, United Kingdom: Routledge, 2016).

36 Login S. George and Crystal L. Park, "Meaning in Life as Comprehension, Purpose, and Mattering: Toward Integration and New Research Questions," *Review of General Psychology* 20, no. 3 (September 2016): pp. 205–220, https://doi.org/10.1037/gpr0000077; Frank Martela and Michael F. Steger, "The Three Meanings of Meaning in Life: Distinguishing Coherence, Purpose, and Significance," *The Journal of Positve Psychology* 11, no. 5 (January 27, 2016): pp. 531–545, https://doi.org/10.1080/17439760.2015.1137623.

EXERCISE

Your purpose in life can change depending on your circumstance, which can be hard to clarify, especially if you are working through a crisis or a traumatic event. The following questions may be helpful for you to consider as you work toward figuring out your purpose or mission.

What are some specific hopes or aims you would like to say you achieved as you get older?

....

....

When you think about those hopes/goals, how to do you envision achieving them?

....

....

What are some core values that you would like to embrace as you move toward achieving these goals?

....

....

What do you think might be some obstacles that would get in the way of your achieving those goals?

....

....

What features of your personality do you think will help you achieve these goals?

....

....

What gives you inspiration when it is difficult to find motivation to achieve your goals?

....

....

If you could achieve anything, what would it be and why?

....

....

What would others say your purpose is on this earth?

_____

_____

EXERCISE

Defining or reevaluating your sense of purpose is one of the most challenging components of building resilience. It can cause you to reevaluate your values in several domains. One simple way to clarify and simplify this is to write down a purpose statement like an organization's mission statement.

A mission statement is typically a formal summary of the goals and objectives of a company, organization, or an individual. Generally speaking, mission statements consist of three parts:

1. An explanation of what you hope to accomplish in your life.
2. A sense of how you envision accomplishing your goals.
3. Highlights of the core values that you aim to live by.

An example of an individual's mission statement might look like this:

> My mission and purpose for my life is to remember that I have endured hardship in my life, and that even though it feels insurmountable at times, I have been able to perservere and be resilient. I hope to be able to achieve prolonged resilience by being introspective and compassionate to myself when things become challenging. I will walk through life with respect and loving kindness toward myself and others.

Here is another example:

> To find fulfillment and happiness in my life, I will participate, with intentionality, in as many life experiences as possible. I will approach these experiences with love and humility, and honor and respect those who are along with me for the journey.

Write your purpose statement below.

My Purpose Statement:

_____

_____

_____

Consider examining your mission statement, a.k.a. your "purpose" statement, every few weeks, especially as you evolve and become more resilient.

EXERCISE

Identifying coherence, your ability to organize and structure your environment in a predictable way so as to make life matter, can be challenging. Answer yes or no to the questions below to evaluate the extent to which you have coherence.

STATEMENT	YES	NO
1. I like routine.	1	0
2. I thrive on change.	0	1
3. I struggle with being flexible.	0	1
4. I find life change to be challenging and a hardship.	0	1
5. I feel that so far, my life is turning out the way I want.	1	0
6. I feel that life has too many obstacles and is challenging.	0	1
7. I like to take risks.	1	0
8. I feel uncomfortable when plans change.	0	1
9. I fear the unknown.	0	1
10. I feel that I am being treated fairly.	1	0
11. I feel as though I care about the things going on around me.	1	0
My Score		

Now, add up the total. If your score totals to more than a 5, you likely have a strong sense of coherence, meaning that your internal world (your mindset) and your external world (the things going on around you) align, which is useful when overcoming life's challenges. Ways to continue to develop your coherence include slowing down and reflecting, putting things into perspective, and further developing your internal locus of control—the belief that you, as opposed to forces beyond your influence, have control over the outcome of the events in your life.

EXERCISE

Explore the questions below to evaluate if you have enough significance or value added to your life. This exercise will help you identify areas for growth.

Why do you get up every morning?

_____

_____

_____

What/who are the reasons that make your life worth living, even through the toughest of times?

_____

_____

_____

Who would miss you—family, friends, colleagues—if you weren't available to them anymore?

_____

_____

_____

Do big life course changes—marriage, divorce, death—make you feel less than?

_____

_____

_____

How do you feel others value you?

_____

_____

_____

Do you feel like you have reached your potential in life?

_____

_____

_____

Do you feel unworthy?

....

....

What would you want people to say about you in a eulogy?

....

....

If you won the lottery, what you would do to impact the world? Name one or two.

....

....

EXERCISE

In Japanese culture, one's *ikigai* is a part of everyday living. It consists of two words: *iki*, which means "life," and *gai*, which describes value or worth. Your ikigai can be thought of as your life's purpose that allows you to have a future vision despite momentary hardship or crisis. Your ikigai consists of four domains—what you love, what you are good at, something the world needs, and something you are paid for. By exploring your ikigai, the hope is that you find a balance of these four domains, allowing you to have a greater sense of meaning and purpose. See the diagram below.[37]

37 Wikimedia Commons, "File: Ikigai-EN.svg," last accessed May 16, 2023, https://commons.wikimedia.org/wiki/File:Ikigai-EN.svg.

For the initial part of this exercise, draw the four circles of the ikigai. In each of the ikigai circles, list: what you love, what you are good at, what the world needs, and what you can be paid for. Try not to overthink your responses.

Once you have completed the first part of this exercise, flip over your paper so you don't see your answers and examine the following questions to help narrow down your initial list within the ikigai.

What you love...

Think about the last time that you were happy/content. What were you doing?

_____

_____

_____

Name the top five experiences/situations that give you pleasure on a consistent basis.

1 _____

2. _____

3. _____

4. _____

5. _____

Name the top five ways to play as an adult that bring you joy.

1 _____

2. _____

3. _____

4. _____

5. _____

What do those who are close to you notice about what brings you the greatest sense of happiness?

_____

_____

_____

_____

What you are good at...

Without overthinking, complete this sentence: I feel efficacious when I...

_____

_____

_____

_____

On a job interview, I like to talk about my skills in these areas (complete a list):

1 _____

2. _____

3. _____

4. _____

5. _____

Others say my top five strengths are:

1 _____

2. _____

3. _____

4. _____

5. _____

When people seek your expertise, what are they typically asking you for help with?

_____

_____

_____

_____

If money, status, and power had no bearing on your job of choice, what would do instead?

_____

_____

_____

_____

What the world needs...

How do you think the world would most benefit from you (your skills, your efforts, your passion etc.)?

_____

_____

_____

_____

Who inspires you and why?

_____

_____

_____

_____

If you had a magic wand, what would you change or do for the world?

_____

_____

_____

_____

THE *resilience* WORKBOOK FOR WOMEN

What you can be paid for...

What do you get paid to do now?

....

....

What do you think people should pay you to do?

....

....

If money didn't matter, what type of work would you do?

....

....

Now on another sheet of paper, draw the four circles of the ikigai. Review and reflect on the diagram having just explored the questions above. Notice if there are any themes or patterns in how you fill in the current circles. See if any of the four domains intersect. Consider any new insights you may have compared to the first ikigai you previously completed. Ask yourself if there are any steps or actions that you may need to take to get you closer to where the four circles of the ikiagi intersect. List potential action steps below:

1 ....

2. ....

3. ....

4. ....

EXERCISE

Now, that you have reviewed, examined, and completed a few exercises on what is understood to be the three pillars of meaning—a sense of purpose, a sense of coherence, and a sense of significance—you may have a better sense of the areas in which you need continued growth. Below is a list of activities that have been found to be helpful in clarifying and growing meaning from experience.

Possible Experiences to Enhance One's Sense of Meaning:

- Foster a passion.
- Volunteer and help others.
- Develop and cultivate social connections.
- Seek/find a sense of belonging in communities that share similar values.
- Practice mindfulness, meditation, yoga, or other exercises helpful with self-regulation.
- Experience moments of beauty and awe.
- Take control of your environment and put into place routines and patterns.

Chapter 4

HOW CONNECTIONS HEAL

*Each friend represents a world in us, a world possibly not born until
they arrive, and it is only by this meeting a new world is born.*

—Anaïs Nin

Humans are hardwired for connection; most likely, without this evolutionary capacity, we would not be where we are today. Data suggests that our social environment profoundly shapes us and that we suffer when those social bonds are threatened or jeopardized.[38] From the earliest points of our evolution, we relied on connection for survival; even today, research indicates that our physical and mental health are highly correlated to positive cultures of connection.[39]

No duh, right? Especially after the global experience of COVID-19, when we were all in and out of periods of isolation. Losing those hard and soft social interactions took a toll on most of us, especially women. A research study by McKinsey indicated that women, in particular mothers and caregivers, were the most adversely impacted by the pandemic as they were tasked with the toughest parts of government shutdowns: caring for the home and caring for and teaching children while also working.[40] The study shared that female-identifying caretakers were more than three times as likely than their male counterparts to bear the burden of home/work responsibilities. While those who were fortunate enough to have some external support in communal and familial arenas fared better, many women survived the pandemic all on their own, utilizing any bits of resilience they could muster. Some women, as you well know, were forced to make excruciating decisions, such as leaving their children in childcare during the height of the pandemic, while others had the privilege of taking a leave from work.

---

38 Matthew D. Lieberman, *Social: Why Our Brains Are Wired to Connect* (Oxford (GB): Oxford University Press, 2015).

39 Karen Feldscher, "Social Connections Boost Resilience among Elderly after Disaster," Harvard Featured News Stories, October 8, 2019, https://www.hsph.harvard.edu/news/features/social-connections-boost-resilience-among-elderly-after-disaster.

40 "Women in the Workplace 2022," McKinsey & Company, October 18, 2022, https://www.mckinsey.com/featured-insights/diversity-and-inclusion/women-in-the-workplace.

We saw people's natural inclination to reach out and touch someone, even if the "touching" was virtual through Zoom, Google Teams, HouseParty, etc., indicating the natural urge to get that support—or to fill up our natural reserves of resilience. Thinking back to this time, albeit it wasn't so long ago, it is pretty remarkable to remember anecdotes about just how meaningful those limited social connections were as they supplanted those day-to-day interactions we formerly valued. I remember narratives in my practice and within my friend circles about the opportunity that the pandemic allowed for the reinvigoration of long-lost friendships and how that was critical to survival for many of us. In several instances, it provided folks with companionship and socio-emotional support. It supplanted that in-person camaraderie that one would otherwise get from small talk around the office water cooler. Several friends and clients noted the profound impact of the absence of in-person connections on their physical and mental health: anxiety, depression, changes in their ability to access language, and lonesomeness.

The significance of such correlations has tremendous backing in the literature. Social epidemiologist Ichiro Kawachi of Harvard documented the need for in-person connection while researching the elderly in Japan following the 2011 earthquake and tsunami.[41] He found that the most crucial factor in disaster resilience was not material resources such as medical supplies, food, or shelter, but social capital. The research demonstrated the importance that social connections and interpersonal relationships hold in terms of improved mental and physical health outcomes. Especially those social relationships that are characterized by a shared sense of identity, norms, values, and reciprocity.

The correlation between diminished health outcomes and decreased social connections makes perfect sense, as our need for social connections/affiliation starts before birth. At birth, we connect with our mothers on a primal level, hence the skin-to-skin contact with our mothers that boosts dopamine, oxytocin, and bonding early on. Data demonstrates that both children and mothers benefit from attunement, as both get that feel-good chemical high.[42]

Children born to mothers who are responsive and attuned tend to be happy despite the stress of life and appear to be more secure adults. That said, it makes sense that there is not only a correlation between social affiliation and happiness later in life but an actual feedback loop between social affiliation and dopamine, and dopamine and one's ability to want to engage with others.[43] The same research indicates that after prolonged isolation, even when there is a longing to connect with others, it can become harder for some to engage in pro-social behavior.

---

[41] Feldscher, "Social Connections Boost Resilience among Elderly after Disaster.

[42] Rafael Franco, Irene Reyes-Resina, and Gemma Navarro, "Dopamine in Health and Disease: Much More than a Neurotransmitter," *Biomedicines* 9, no. 2 (January 22, 2021): p. 109, https://doi.org/10.3390/biomedicines9020109; L. Strathearn, "Maternal Neglect: Oxytocin, Dopamine and the Neurobiology of Attachment," *Journal of Neuroendocrinology* 23, no. 11 (October 18, 2011): pp. 1054–1065, https://doi.og/101111/j.1365-2826.2011.02228.x.

[43] Gillian A. Matthews et al., "Dorsal Raphe Dopamine Neurons Represent the Experience of Social Isolation," *Cell* 164, no. 4 (February 2016): pp. 617–631, https://doi.org/10.1016/j.cell.2015.12.040.

That said, connection and social affiliation are core necessities regardless of when we are having a challenging time. Any connection, irrespective of whether it is someone with whom you are closely connected or a stranger, can give a surge of much-needed oxytocin—commonly referred to as the love hormone—to strengthen one's resilience and plow ahead.[44] Even connections on a micro-level, such as a gaze, the sound of a voice, or touch, can give one the boost to be slightly more resilient.

Consider the case of Peg.

CASE SCENARIO

Peg came into treatment just as she was approaching retirement. She had spent 30 years working at the same company, and while she had made close work friends over the years, many of them retired, passed away, or left the company altogether. Peg was starting to feel anxious about her pending retirement as she was already feeling isolated—a few years prior, her long-term partner had passed away.

Unfortunately, just as Peg had started working with me around her anxiety about this issue, the pandemic hit. As an older woman in New York City's outer boroughs, Peg's anxiety substantially increased. She retired earlier than expected, and in retirement, she experienced chronic health problems and bouts of loneliness. Her plans to take up tennis and piano lessons and travel independently came to a complete halt. Like many of us during that time, Peg suffered from ambiguous loss as she had not received the retirement send-off that she had hoped for and was unable to get any closure to that part of her life. Peg's anxieties soon transformed into lethargy and depression.

While our weekly phone sessions were helpful and undoubtedly gave Peg a short-lived dopamine boost, they didn't quite do the trick. We discussed strategies to alleviate some of the depression and lonesomeness. Would Peg be willing to do an outdoor yoga program? Participate in a Zoom meeting with the local community center? Have a walking and talking date with a former colleague, or even venture to meet me so we could do a walking and talking session together? Rightly so, Peg wasn't ready to risk social connection in the wake of a global pandemic. She tried to utilize social media as best she could to reach out to people from her past with whom she had lost contact. Even though she was able to revitalize some of these connections, her experience with Instagram and Facebook wasn't enough for her. Often these social interactions were inconsistent—sometimes, an online conversation would go on for hours, and then there would be no follow-through. This experience would leave her crestfallen.

Despite my coaxing, Peg did take up one suggestion: to get a cat. During our sessions, Peg and I talked about our shared love for animals and how my dog Luna had provided me with

---

44 Ruth Feldman, "Oxytocin and Social Affiliation in Humans," *Hormones and Behavior* 61, no. 3 (March 2012): pp. 380–391, https://doi.org/10.1016/j.yhbeh.2012.01.008.

significant comfort and buoyancy to face the unknown. One day after a session, Peg met with a neighbor who had advertised needing homes for kittens, and just like that, Noma, Peg's new cat, arrived on her doorstep. Peg's mood improved dramatically—no surprise here as Noma gave Peg a new purpose, lots of oxytocin-filled cuddles, and a new meaning to this chapter in her life. Ironically, in the end, Noma's presence not only created a sense of purpose and significance in Peg's life but ultimately forced Peg (and Noma) to make more in-person connections as visits to the pet store became the norm, as did visits to Noma's vet. Now, Peg has two cats, Norm, and Noma, and volunteers at her local non-kill animal shelter. Peg has also cultivated a closer and, as she puts it, more "meaningful" Instagram community that focuses on their pets.

The case example of Peg demonstrates that when we experience a sense of connection, warmth, and positive emotion, whether it is from another human or an animal, we are bolstering our resilience, even if on a small level. The truth is that sometimes we look to the clear places for connections—family or friends. But as we know, sometimes these connections aren't helpful or even available. Often, we neglect to consider those connections around us that are less obvious and that add meaning and resiliency to our lives. Remember, as the research indicates, any connection can help promote resilience.

Consider the Case of Val.

CASE SCENARIO

Val, a zennial (someone who was born between the early 1990s and the early 2000s) moved to New York City in the pandemic's aftermath. Val had grown up in a small Iowa town and longed to live in a big city. Although several of her friends from college had followed suit, the stint was short lived for most of them. Unfortunately, when Val arrived in NYC, she was alone. Sadly, Val was not met with the social engagements, the brunches, and the other activities she hoped for.

Working from her tiny apartment did not afford her the opportunity for the classic water cooler chats and work-sponsored happy hours. Val was experiencing a significant bout of loneliness and uncertainty about herself and her decision. But things turned around for Val when she started going to a small workout studio. Initially, she sat in the back—slightly out of practice socially (note that this limitation was self-reported)—and after a few sessions, the trainer noticed her and encouraged her to move up a row. The trainer continued to notice her efforts each week and invited her to move to the front row and try different challenges.

Whatever the motivation for the trainer, this contact was a massive game changer for Val. Even though many of us may see this as minimal, such a micro-connection for Val not only gave her something to look forward to but it correlated with her experience of reduced stress at work and improvements in her self-esteem and other social connections.

We need to notice, acknowledge, and reflect on how small interactions impact us and foster a greater sense of resilience. As previously noted, we tend to focus on friends and familial relationships to provide emotional support when we encounter periods of difficulty. Often, we either neglect or forget those micro-moments of connection with others.

For this exercise, complete the following weeklong calendar by identifying any micro-moments of connection that may have occurred and how they made you feel. This exercise may be more challenging for some than others, so I recommend starting with today and then filling out the week as necessary. You can look at the example below. (Note: I always recommend that people complete exercises in an old-school way with a pen and paper, as some research suggests that it helps create and strengthen neuroplasticity.)[45]

	MORNING	MIDDAY	AFTERNOON	EVENING
MONDAY	**Interaction:** Small interaction with the cashier lady at the store. **Feeling:** Positive	**Interaction:** Nice couple talked to me in the elevator. **Feeling:** Warm, hopeful, overall positive.	**Interaction:** Someone asked me about where I bought my scarf. **Feeling:** Seen, acknowledged, confident.	**Interaction:** Stranger complimented me on my well-trained dog. **Feeling:** Humored, flattered.

Complete your own below:

Beginning Date: ....

	MORNING	MIDDAY	AFTERNOON	EVENING
MONDAY	Interaction: Feeling:	Interaction: Feeling:	Interaction: Feeling:	Interaction: Feeling:

---

45 Deborah Ross and Kathleen Adams, *Your Brain on Ink: A Workbook on Neuroplasticity and the Journal Ladder* (Lanham, MD: Rowman & Littlefield, 2016), 68–72.

	MORNING	MIDDAY	AFTERNOON	EVENING
TUESDAY	Interaction: Feeling:	Interaction: Feeling:	Interaction: Feeling:	Interaction: Feeling:
WEDNESDAY	Interaction: Feeling:	Interaction: Feeling:	Interaction: Feeling:	Interaction: Feeling:
THURSDAY	Interaction: Feeling:	Interaction: Feeling:	Interaction: Feeling:	Interaction: Feeling:
FRIDAY	Interaction: Feeling:	Interaction: Feeling:	Interaction: Feeling:	Interaction: Feeling:

THE *resilience* **WORKBOOK** FOR WOMEN

	MORNING	MIDDAY	AFTERNOON	EVENING
SATURDAY	Interaction: Feeling:	Interaction: Feeling:	Interaction: Feeling:	Interaction: Feeling:
SUNDAY	Interaction: Feeling:	Interaction: Feeling:	Interaction: Feeling:	Interaction: Feeling:

Can you document your micro-moments of connection regularly? Try this exercise for at least a week. There is no pressure to have a micro-moment reflected for all the columns or at the set intervals. The hope and goals are to be more mindful of when these opportunities occur and recognize how they make you feel.

EXERCISE

While this exercise is basic, many people find it helpful to map out their web of social connections and identify how useful they will be (or at least how you hope them to be) in supporting you when you experience hardship. Complete the map below with your name located in the center circle. Add extensions to the web as needed. In each bubble, name a person from your social network (familial and nonfamilial) and scale your perceived helpfulness of them from 1 to 5, with a 1 indicating that they would provide you with the least support and a 5 indicating that they would be very supportive. Those that score higher are those who are your encouragers!

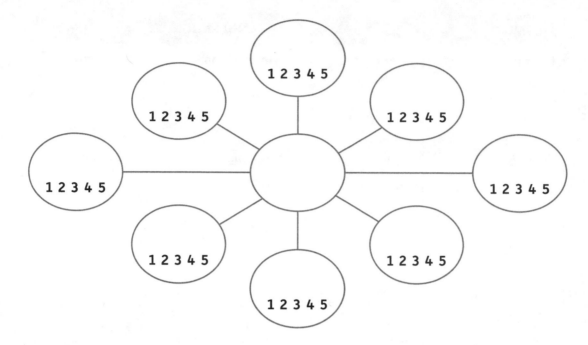

It is important to remember that you are scaling the helpfulness of these individuals as it relates to your current issue. Some people in your social web may be more helpful/supportive for certain problems than others. For those you deem to be very helpful, these will be your go-to people from whom to get support. Be mindful not to place all your needs on one person as it may be too overwhelming for them—our supports may experience vicarious trauma or burnout if we overutilize them.

EXERCISE

Considering those in your social network who may help bolster your resilience, reflect on the following questions that may help connect or reconnect with them.

Name three people identified in the exercise above that you would feel comfortable connecting with:

1. ....

2. ....

3. ....

Name three actionable ways that you can connect with each of these individuals:

Person 1:

1. ....

2. ....

3. ....

Person 2:

1. ....

2. ....

3. ....

Person 3:

1. ....

2. ....

3. ....

Name three people identified in the exercise above that evoke positive feelings within you:

1. ....

2. ....

3. ....

Name three actionable ways that you can connect with each of these individuals:

Person 1:

1. ....

2. ....

3. ....

Person 2:

1. ....

2. ....

3. ....

Person 3:

1. ....

2. ....

3. ....

Do any of the individuals mentioned above overlap? If so, consider connecting to that individual first.

Identify a plan to connect with each person within the next month. If you are slightly resistant to reaching out, come up with some ways to motivate yourself!

CONNECTING WITH HEALING COMMUNITIES

Healing communities can help to provide a safe and therapeutic way to receive support, guidance, and connection to boost resilience. Research on trauma survivors has found that communities of group support, especially for women, have been critical in ameliorating the impacts of trauma such as PTSD.[46] More specifically, a plethora of research suggests that women's support groups substantially impact members' mental health, ability to self-regulate, social networks, and sense of empowerment in a positive way. Take, for instance, the power of domestic violence support groups that allow women to connect with and get support from others in a similar situation.

Such support groups allow participants to speak openly and freely with other women who are also experiencing domestic violence and can listen in a nonjudgmental way. Support groups like this can often help women share ideas and strategies about safety and rebuilding their lives when they decide to leave an abusive relationship. Furthermore, this research also suggests that group/community support promotes individual resilience and has a reciprocal relationship with the individual and their other networks. Essentially, the more resilient the individual, the more resilient their romantic partners, family members, neighborhoods, and workplaces.[47]

Moreover, formal or informal group support can help most of us get through some of the most challenging parts of our lives. Being part of a club or a tribe where you are understood can cause the release of oxytocin and boost dopamine.

---

46 Scott M. Hyman, Steven N. Gold, and Melissa A. Cott, "Forms of Social Support That Moderate PTSD in Childhood Sexual Abuse Survivors," *Journal of Family Violence* 18, no. 5 (2003): pp. 295–30, https://doi.org/10.1023/A:1025117311660.

47 Leslie M. Tutty, Bruce A. Bidgood, and Michael A. Rothery, "Support Groups for Battered Women: Research on Their Efficacy," *Journal of Family Violence* 8, no. 4 (December 1993): pp. 325–343, https://doi.org/10.1007/bf00978097; Lauren M. Sippel et al., "How Does Social Support Enhance Resilience in the Trauma-Exposed Individual?," *Ecology and Society* 20, no. 4 (2015), https/doi.org/10.5751/es-07832-200410.

While group support around trauma and trauma recovery can be a more obvious way for women to grow their resilience, the example of Ann below shows the variety of ways in which we can benefit from group support.

CASE SCENARIO

Ann, a 65-year-old female on the verge of retirement, was hoping to lose weight to manage her diabetes and rheumatoid arthritis. Ann joined Weight Watchers to gain some support and accountability in her efforts. Regularly, Ann participated in the programs, including their in-person and online support group. Through the group, Ann was not only able to listen to other women's stories of successful weight loss and get validation for her weight-loss wins, but she was also able to get a new relatable social network. After a short time participating in a hybrid model of the group, Ann was able to elevate some of these relationships outside of the group by texting and calling new friends. She started by casually requesting recipes and advice, and her engagement was well received. Ann began inviting people over for potlucks and cooking classes and, as a result, developed more intimate relationships. Eventually, Ann had a newer, more diverse community of women from whom she could gain support and validation in times of need.

EXERCISE

While you may have identified those individuals who are your supports, it is also helpful to determine your current communities for healing and other purposes in your life. Complete the list below and identify which communities may benefit you with your everyday needs.

FORMAL COMMUNITY	INFORMAL COMMUNITY
Examples: Divorce support group, NAMI, etc.	Examples: Band, cross-fit, running club, etc.

Which of these communities do you feel will most understand you and enhance your sense of strength and resilience? Why?

....

....

....

....

EXERCISE

Indeed, a component of connecting with communities of other people is the fact that you may have to get comfortable with the uncomfortable. As clichéd as this saying is, it is true. Even if you are feeling especially vulnerable right now, a formal or informal community may aid your resiliency. Take a moment to reflect on if there are other communities you think would be helpful for you. Are there other communities you may want to connect with but have yet to do so? If yes, consider answering these questions:

Name three barriers that are keeping you from connecting with these communities:

1. ....

2. ....

3. ....

Name three motivators that would help you connect with these communities:

1. ....

2. ....

3. ....

What is the scariest part of trying to connect with these communities?

....

....

What are you most hopeful about regarding these communities?

....

....

THE *resilience* WORKBOOK FOR WOMEN

SOCIAL MEDIA: A TOOL FOR CONNECTION, COMMUNITY, AND RESILIENCE

This workbook would be remiss if it did not discuss the role and importance of connecting people to communities, especially healing groups, using social media. As evidenced by how we communicated during the COVID-19 pandemic, social media, such as Instagram, Tik-Tok, Twitter, Facebook (Meta), and other networking apps allow us to connect with our existing social networks and develop newer ones. Through the use of social media, the old adage of "find your people" is more possible now than ever before. The role of social media in supporting resilience during the pandemic or natural disasters cannot be underestimated.[48] During the pandemic, it was a critical tool for many, especially those isolated and located in more remote regions, to restore or replace invaluable in-person human connections.

Let's examine the data to get a clearer sense of social media's profound impact and influence on building resilience. As of fall 2022, there were 4.74 billion people actively using social media.[49] In 2019, 72 percent of American adults living in the United States used at least one social media platform.[50] Over 50 percent of teen users reported using social media to help them get through hard times, while about seven out of 10 adults in the United States use social media for a variety of reasons, including social engagement, enhancement, and maintaining interpersonal connections.[51] Teenage girls and adult women were more likely than their male counterparts to use social media in a social way to curate and maintain relationships with their friends, family, and romantic partners.[52]

As the data suggests, most of us have experienced the beauty of the dopamine hit that comes with DMs, liking, and commenting on other people's posts. Indeed, while living in isolation, many reported that engagement with social media decreased feelings of depression and loneliness while

---

48 Rita Mano, "Social Media and Resilience in the COVID-19 Crisis," *Advances in Applied Sociology* 10, no. 11 (2020): pp. 454–464, https://doi.org/10.4236/aasoci.2020.1011026; Magali Reghezza-Zitt and Samuel Rufat, "Disentangling the Range of Responses to Threats, Hazards, and Disasters. Vulnerability, Resilience, and Adaptation in Question," *Cybergeo*, September 3, 2019, https://doi.org/10.4000/cybergeo.32917.

49 SMPerth, "2023 Social Media Statistics," March 8, 2022, https://www.smperth.com/resources/social-media-statistics.

50 Mano, "Social Media and Resilience in the COVID-19 Crisis"; Reghezza-Zitt and Rufat, "Disentangling the Range of Responses to Threats, Hazards, and Disasters."

51 Monica Anderson, "Teens, Social Media and Technology 2018," Pew Research Center: Internet, Science & Tech (Pew Research Center, August 10, 2022), https://www.pewresearch.org/internet/2018/05/31/teens-social-media-technology-2018; Amanda Lenhart, "Teens, Social Media & Technology Overview 2015," *Pew Research Center: Internet, Science & Tech* (Pew Research Center, August 10, 2022), https://www.pewresearch.org/internet/2015/04/09/teens-social-media-technology-2015.

52 Lenhart, "Teens, Social Media & Technology Overview 2015"; Jennifer Conway, "The Fairest Facebook Users: Women Logging in More Often Than Men, Study Finds," Business Wire, October 4, 2012, https://www.businesswire.com/news/home/20121004005734/en/The-Fairest-Facebook-Users-Women-Logging-in-More-Often-Than-Men-Study-Finds.

increasing self-esteem each time a new follower was added, or a distant connection liked a picture. Our engagement with social media can have tremendous benefits for our health, well-being, and resilience. As we know, engaging with social media can not only expand the depth and breadth of our connections at the moment but also can foster a more expansive social network once a crisis is over.[53]

Read on for how it impacted Kristen.

CASE SCENARIO

Kristen had been contemplating divorce when she came in for therapy. She was in her mid-50s and worked a high-power job at a corporate consulting firm. She and her partner had decided early on that he would be the primary caretaker of their two children, who were in high school. Kristen had started to feel disillusioned and disconnected from everyone—her kids, her husband, her friends. On a more extended work trip, she met a fellow female colleague—Stacey—who was her "mirror" image.

After Kristen's work trip ended and she was placed at another location, she maintained her friendship with Stacey. When not working or trying to tap into her very busy family, Kristen frequently tapped into Stacey. At first, it was every day; then, it was multiple times a day. They would DM back and forth, discussing challenges they were having with their partners and children, chatting about new music and clothing trends, and even commiserating with one another about their shared bouts with Lyme disease.

Over time, Kristen's tapping into Stacey became an hourly occurrence. Kristen and Stacey started to connect and "friend" one another's Instagram community, broadening each other's social network. Kristen's anxiety and desire to separate from her husband seemed to vanish even though she remained geographically distant from her children and her husband. Citing this new friendship as a "breath of fresh air" and having a new friend forum where she could be seen, Kristen appeared to be thriving. The connections and communications with Stacey and this new community provided Kristen with the dopamine high that she needed to stay buoyant in her "real life."

Things continued to go well for the friendship between Kristen and Stacey for a long while until one day, Kristen noticed that the cadence with which she and Stacey communicated slowed down. In calls or sessions, Kristen would vocalize her worry about what was going on—questioning if she had done or said something wrong or offended someone in their (now) expansive online social network. Although Kristen did her best to figure out what had changed, Stacey cited that she was just too busy to communicate as often.

Stacey further shared that she was trying to spend more time with her family and children before they went to college and had decided to "slow" down her use of social media after one

---

53 Mano, "Social Media and Resilience in the COVID-19 Crisis."

of her kids had complained that she was always on the phone. Kristen was devastated and tried to replicate the friendship with others in their social network, but nothing much came to fruition.

Unfortunately, in Kristen's case, we see the pros and cons of using social media for connection. The ease of connecting with Stacey in the initial phase provided Kristen with the much-needed support, validation, encouragement, and friendship to get through a difficult period in her midlife. As witnessed, Kristen's initial interactions with Stacey likely served to replicate what a friendship between two middle-aged women would be like; however, it evolved to an extension of what may have happened if they had met in person and socialized regularly. The hitch here is that since Kristen and Stacey's communication with one other was online, thus their friendship was stripped of its real-world limits. In the real world, would two busy mothers with high-power consulting jobs be able to communicate as frequently? Probably not. The painful part of this experience for Kristen and others who overuse social media for connection is that the sudden disengagement from an online friend does feel like real-world rejection. The sudden dopamine deficit that occurs when you can't reach back out or chat with the person manifests in the brain, similar to depression and anxiety, and can have similar symptomology.[54]

EXERCISE

When building out a social network or connecting to healing communities online, there should be a balance. Even if you cannot replicate your online relationships in person, assessing and recognizing your relationship with social media is essential. The disappointment that can occur can be profound, especially if you are more vulnerable.

Answer the following questions to understand how healthy your relationship is with social media and your online social network.

Approximately how many social media platforms are you using and how many hours a day do you use these platforms?

Are you an active or a passive user?

How often do you have meaningful and pleasureable contact with others?

---

54 "Social Media, Dopamine, and Stress: Converging Pathways," *Dartmouth Undergraduate Journal of Science*, accessed April 4, 2023, https://sites.dartmouth.edu/dujs/2022/08/20/social-media-dopamine-and-stress-converging-pathways.

What do others think of your social media usage?

Are your connections on social media mostly those you met online?

Do you get the same or greater pleasure in activities that do not involve your participation in social media?

Are the conversations on social media reciprocal?

How do you feel when an online connection ghosts you or doesn't demonstrate a sufficient responsiveness to your messages/likes/images, etc.?

Can you trust that these online connections will be there for you in times of great need?

Whom would you reach out to before your involvement with social media? Would you reach out to them now if you were in a pinch?

Upon reflection, how healthy do you feel your relationship is with social media and your online network?

What are some things you would like to modify/change about your relationship with social media and your online network?

_____

_____

_____

_____

_____

EXERCISE

A reality check on your relationship with social media and your virtual community and its impact on your resilience may have you reconsidering a way to find more balance. Below is a list of some ways that you may be able to incorporate more balance in your real and virtual worlds.

Unfollow the unhealthy. Take notice of how you feel after engaging with the content on specific social media platforms. Do you find yourself unable to disengage? Do you feel yourself feeling less than others, fighting off comparison fatigue? If so, unfollow and block anything that stirs up bad vibes. Tune in to the positive.

Finding and fostering your tribe. Search for digital communities that have similar interests and values to you. If something doesn't feel right, pay attention to your intuition, and move on.

Mindful mentions. Slow down and practice intentionality with what you post. Think about the content and if it is an accurate portrayal of you and your values. Is it a positive contribution? Note that sometimes in the Meta universe, things _are_ permanent.

Time tracking. Track your time on your electronic device and where you spend your time. Research indicates that people spend at least two hours a day on social media; however, it is likely more. Utilize the time tracking tools provided by the various platforms. Try to integrate your free time with online and in-person engagements.

Compassion breaks. Too much time on social media can take away from your daily activities of living, and in the age of 24/7 communication, it can also be hard to step back completely. Whether you do a social detox or a mini vacation from social, it may be helpful to set a concrete goal and time frame for this and log out of all your accounts. Seek out someone who can encourage you and keep you accountable if you struggle with the willpower to do it alone.

COMPANY WE SHOULD CHOOSE TO KEEP

Regardless of the community—in person or virtual—it is important to take stock of whether it is the right community for you to foster your resilience. Sometimes we may enter a formal group that we think will enhance our sense of resilience, only to learn that it reinforces the same narrative we are working on rewriting. As noted, there is value in being with others who may have lived through or resolved a dilemma or experience close to our own. While this is the beauty of self-help groups, it is important to recognize the likely reality that when most of us decide to participate in a self-help group, we might be in the depths of our darkest moments. Motivation to participate in a group can stem from the self-awareness that we have done the negative narrative loop-de-loop for the millionth time, or maybe a friend pointed out their frustration with our constant negativity, prompting the need to do something about it.

Such newfound self-reflection may have persuaded you to purchase this workbook. Perhaps, this awareness caused you to dedicate an entire weekend scouring the internet for the appropriate self-help group. Nonetheless, your need for support brought you to this pivotal moment where you are willing to take a risk, connect with strangers, and muster the courage to bare your naked, raw, messy, distraught self. So, let's be crystal clear—the group you select needs to be the right one for you. There's a lot on the line. Consider the case of Patty.

CASE SCENARIO

Patty initially came in for therapy after it was suggested by three sources: her acupuncturist, her best friend, and her general practitioner. Patty had been complaining about digestive issues, chronic headaches, and a "frog" in her throat for as long as she could remember. For years, Patty sought a traditional medical explanation for her pains, but to no avail. By the time Patty came to meet me, she was at her wit's end and ready to do whatever was needed to end her bodily pain.

Identifying as an older, cisgender, Irish Catholic originating from Boston, Patty had never sought out therapy before, nor did she believe in its effectiveness. One of her first questions was, "Do you think *you* will be able to help *me*?" I noted that her skepticism was, to some extent, reasonable. Therapy isn't a magic bullet, and much to my chagrin, I don't have a magic wand. Nonetheless, sitting before me was this woman 30 years my senior whose symptoms likely outdated my age; I had a job to do even if we were both dubious about the outcome.

As we started our work together and Patty's narrative unfolded, I learned she had a great deal of relational trauma. She was born into a very traditional Irish Catholic Bostonian family and grew up in the forties. Her mother was a homemaker for most of her life until her father's death, and her father worked as a longshoreman on the docks of the Boston Harbor. According to Patty, her father worked long hours and often went to the local bars after work. Her mother often recruited Patty or one of her seven siblings to find her father on payday to get his check before he bought beer rounds for locals at the pub.

Managing eight children while Patty's father was off at work was challenging for her mother, who suffered from bouts of depression. Often Patty was left to her own devices and endured a tremendous amount of physical abuse from her brothers. This went unaddressed until Patty was able to leave the house at 17 years old, when she married her husband.

It became clear that when 17-year-old Patty met her 25-year-old husband Declan, she had instilled all her hopes, her sense of safety, and her identity into the marriage, and subsequently, into raising her son. There were not many rays of sunshine in Patty's narrative, at least not as she initially spoke of her story. Patty further shared that after a decade of marriage, she had enough of Declan's overindulging in drugs and alcohol (like her father), and his mismanaging the family's finances, which nearly put the family in financial ruin. As the stress of the marriage ensued, we later learned that was also the onset of many of her complaints about how she was feeling physically.

Like a good Irish Catholic girl of her time, Patty consulted with her priest, who reiterated that divorce was condemned and advised that she should "pull up her big girl pants and soldier on—her circumstance was typical." Patty did just that—for another decade. She soldiered on until one day, she learned that her husband of 15 years had been duplicitous and had another family. Furious and filled with contempt, Patty ended the marriage. The church would not grant her an annulment and because of being "divorced," Patty felt very ostracized from her church community.

Needing to find a new anchor, Patty discovered a local group of divorced mothers who would meet as a formal group weekly and informally with one another. As Patty portrayed, the group organizer was very like-minded and simpatico. In fact, from Patty's perspective, most of the mothers in the group, like her, experienced very traumatic divorces that ended in infidelity. They jokingly referred to themselves as the "Misandrist Mothers Club." One of them even went so far as to suggest they have T-shirts made up with that logo—Patty protested, reminding the other mothers that she had a son whom she loved and respected.

In spite of my shame about not knowing what misandrist meant, I went ahead and looked it up. For the record, a misandrist is defined as a person who hates men. Then, just like I turned on a 1000-watt light bulb, everything made sense to me. Patty was not in a healthy, productive group for her or for what I suspected she had wanted. With much trepidation, I presented my hypothesis that Patty's support group didn't do much supporting; in its man-bashing, the group kept a dominant, unhealthy narrative alive that all men were terrible, dirty cheaters. In this case, the group's negativity was causing her a significant amount of internal, unidentified stress and dissonance, resulting in her bodily complaints.

Recognizing that this group was toxic, Patty disengaged from the formal group and maintained a few healthier one-on-one relationships. She worked on looking for female role models whose goals were to move forward, re-partner, and bring positivity to their lives. Once Patty could do this, there was almost a complete reduction in her bodily complaints. A few years ago, Patty let me know that she is now happily re-partnered with a man who experienced a similar divorce story.

The best lesson learned here is negativity begets negativity. When trying to move forward in creating our new narrative, we must have the correct type of prosocial support so as not to reinforce those strong NUTs. Once Patty was able to surround herself with others who were successfully able to let go of their negativity and author more meaningful and loving narratives, she could do the same. Patty allowed herself to be open-minded enough to try a new group and connect with those who let go of their negative thoughts and embraced the positivity of their new situation. As psychiatrist and philosopher David Hawkins posits, such ability is reflective of the transfer of one's positive energy, which activates another's latent sense of positivity, allowing change by what we colloquially refer to as "getting it through osmosis."[55]

EXERCISE

As with Patty's experience, it is essential to highlight the features of healthy group dynamics and provide a schematic to discern if a group is a good enough fit for you and your needs. Remember that lists and assessment tools are guides; it is critically important that you pay close attention to your intuition and your gut. Patty had not been completely at ease with her group, but fear of breaking the group cohesion by exiting kept her stuck and resulted in her somatic complaints.

Score each of the features of a healthy healing community on a scale of 1 to 5, with 1 being poor and 5 being superior. The outcome of this assessment may clarify if this is a good group dynamic for you.

KEY FEATURES OF A HEALTHY GROUP	POOR	FAIR	AVERAGE	GOOD	EXCELLENT
How strong is the feeling of physical and emotional safety within your community?	1	2	3	4	5

---

55 David R. Hawkins, *Letting Go: The Pathway of Surrender* (Carlsbad, CA: Hay House, Inc., 2018).

KEY FEATURES OF A HEALTHY GROUP	POOR	FAIR	AVERAGE	GOOD	EXCELLENT
How strongly do you believe your contribution to the community helps bring you a sense of purpose and belonging?	1	2	3	4	5
In your community, to what degree is kindness, respect, and open and honest communication valued?	1	2	3	4	5
Do you feel as though your participation in the community is welcomed and appreciated?	1	2	3	4	5
Do you feel as though your input and ideas in the community are valued?	1	2	3	4	5
How do you assess your community's capacity to provide its members a sense of belonging, safety, kindness, and appreciation?	1	2	3	4	5
Is mutuality and reciprocity a value of this community?	1	2	3	4	5

Adapted from Virgil Stucker and Associates Blog; https://www.stuckersmithweatherly.com

GET YOUR PLAY ON!

Most children are exposed to multiple play communities as they grow. Our first community of play may be familial—playing games of "school" or "house" with our siblings, cousins, or others with whom we live. As we develop, we may encounter other communities of play through daycare, school, after-school activities, neighbors, and community centers. And then, something significant happens, and we stop engaging in play as we did as children. Adults tend to move closer to more performative types of play, such as engaging in competitive sports, reading, doing a hobby, socializing, or hanging out. Many adults would not even conceive of the above types of play as play but would likely rationalize/

categorize them as something else, such as exercise, personal development, community building, relaxing, etc.

While play can mean different things to different people, I have often found that people who integrate some type of play into their lives tend to be happier and more resilient. Those that incorporate play with community tend to feel and fair better when new challenges arise. Research indicates that playing with at least one other person (and some toys, which we will cover in just a second) increases happiness as an antidepressant.[56]

The science behind how playmates and toys result in happier adults comes from the work of Marian Diamond, a professor at the University of California, Berkeley, and one of the world's leading researchers on neuroplasticity. Realizing that rats have similar neurological development to humans, Diamond and her research team placed three groups of rats into three different environments. All environments had food and water. The "enriched" space had other rats—the "friends" in this situation—and toys; another environment had "friends" and no toys; and the third environment had just a single rat with no toys.

After the experiment, the researchers examined the rats' brains and learned that rats with toys to play with and their rat "friends" in their environment had thicker cerebral cortexes with more neural connections than other rats.[57] In rats and humans, the cerebral cortex is the area of the brain responsible for cognitive processing, attention, and awareness. The research indicated that the development of these new neurological connections in rats with their "friends" and toys was fairly quick, approximately two months. Diamond's research suggests that if humans can also enrich their environments with the presence of toys and playmates, we can generate improved cognitive processing and increase levels of dopamine—begging the question, why don't we spend more time and effort as adult women playing with playmates? It is a no-brainer if you ask me. Consider the case of Jules.

CASE SCENARIO

Jules came into bereavement counseling after Don, her husband of two years, passed away following a sudden heart attack after working out at a local gym one evening. Jules and Don had met at this gym, and his passing on was sudden and unexpected. The loss of Don was crushing for Jules and the entire community. Following his passing, Jules, like many bereaved widows, cloistered up in her home. Occasionally she would entertain visitors, but this wasn't often. Jules's family and employer were increasingly concerned about her mental health. Jules was very resistant to participating in bereavement groups and truly wanted the pain of her loss to be over.

---

56 Elisha Goldstein, *Uncovering Happiness: Overcoming Depression with Mindfulness and Self-Compassion* (New York: Atria Books, 2016).

57 Marian Cleeves Diamond, *Enriching Heredity: The Impact of the Environment on the Anatomy of the Brain* (London: Collier Macmillan, 1988).

While, unfortunately, it isn't realistic to set a timestamp on the end of one's grief for a loved one, Jules and I discussed how one key ingredient might be play. Initially, Jules balked at this—as she was a corporate attorney who, before her bereavement, hardly found time to participate in a semi regular date night with her husband. Jules also felt that it would be inappropriate for her to forgo mourning so soon and had concerns about how her in-laws would perceive her if she suddenly started laughing and having fun again.

After a long weekend, Jules came into my office and had discovered what she thought was revelatory in her healing. Jules shared that her sister had asked her to watch her two young nephews. What surprised Jules about this otherwise typical family favor was how much *fun* she had with her nephews—playing board games, playing catch with the dog, and giggling nonstop. It's not surprising that there was a new inner glow when I saw Jules on that Monday.

Taking my suggestion to go have fun and play, Jules spent more time with her nephews. She set up a weekly time each Saturday when she would relieve her younger sister and watch her sons and dog for a few hours. Play consisted of tag, soccer, and frisbee. Jules was surprised when her sister casually asked her if watching the boys and playing with them each weekend was too much for her. "No way," Jules retorted. She hadn't remembered having this much carefree fun since she was a kid.

Jules's narrative is why play is so healing and even more powerful when you have some playmates, even if they are some young people in your life. Jules's ability to be present in the moment and carefree is demonstrative of something known as a flow state, where you are entirely enthralled and engrossed in something that brings you pleasure and satisfaction, regardless of the goal.

EXERCISE

Find a comfortable place to sit and relax. Close your eyes or find a fixed spot in the room where your eyes can gaze if you don't feel comfortable closing your eyes. Take a few deep breaths and imagine when you were a child. First, imagine when you were 5 years old, 10 years old, 13 years old, and 18 years old.

What do you remember about how you would play at those ages? Note anything that comes to your mind about the play. Try to remember how it made your body feel. Were there any toys or playmates present?

5 years old:

....

....

....

10 years old:

....

....

13 years old:

....

....

18 years old:

....

....

This exercise is tangential to the one above. It asks how you play now, who your playmates are, and which play toys you use now that you are an adult.

How do you play now?

....

....

....

What activities and with whom do you feel the most free-spirited and reinvigorated when you're playing?

....

....

....

Maybe you can play with them more often!

If you are looking for new ways to play and build a new adult play community, look at the list below. You will have the opportunity to rate the degree to which you experience pleasure from the type of play and if you would be willing to engage in this type of play with others.

The list includes play ideas for yourself, but don't forget that having a playmate provides added support for increasing your resilience. In the empty spaces at the bottom of the table, list any other fun or engaging activities that this list might not have included that you might like to enjoy with someone else.

TYPE OF PLAY	FREQUENCY	DEGREE OF PLEASURE (1=LOW; 5=HIGH)	WOULD YOU DO THIS ACTIVITY WITH OTHERS?
Tour a museum			☐ Y ☐ N
Go to a comedy performance			☐ Y ☐ N
Participate in a book club			☐ Y ☐ N
Go see a play			☐ Y ☐ N
Go to a lecture			☐ Y ☐ N
Go to a concert			☐ Y ☐ N
Go to a sporting event			☐ Y ☐ N
Try a new restaurant			☐ Y ☐ N
Take a dance class			☐ Y ☐ N
Go shopping			☐ Y ☐ N
Sing karaoke			☐ Y ☐ N
Go to a craft fair			☐ Y ☐ N
Visit the aquarium or zoo			☐ Y ☐ N
Swim at the beach			☐ Y ☐ N
Hike the mountains			☐ Y ☐ N
Ski/snowboard			☐ Y ☐ N

TYPE OF PLAY	FREQUENCY	DEGREE OF PLEASURE (1=LOW; 5=HIGH)	WOULD YOU DO THIS ACTIVITY WITH OTHERS?
Have a picnic or BBQ			☐ Y ☐ N
Snorkel/waterski/scuba dive			☐ Y ☐ N
Canoe/kayak			☐ Y ☐ N
Sail/boat			☐ Y ☐ N
Fish			☐ Y ☐ N
Bike			☐ Y ☐ N
Jog/Walk			☐ Y ☐ N
Play tennis			☐ Y ☐ N
Golf			☐ Y ☐ N
Rock climb			☐ Y ☐ N
Sing in a choir			☐ Y ☐ N
Birdwatch			☐ Y ☐ N
Vacation			☐ Y ☐ N
Do yoga			☐ Y ☐ N
Cook			☐ Y ☐ N
Have a party			☐ Y ☐ N
Participate in a wine tasting/ cooking class			☐ Y ☐ N
Host a talent show			☐ Y ☐ N
Complete a puzzle			☐ Y ☐ N
Play card games (charades, Taboo, etc.)			☐ Y ☐ N
Play croquet			☐ Y ☐ N

THE *resilience* WORKBOOK FOR WOMEN

TYPE OF PLAY	FREQUENCY	DEGREE OF PLEASURE (1=LOW; 5=HIGH)	WOULD YOU DO THIS ACTIVITY WITH OTHERS?
Listen to music			☐ Y ☐ N
Make/perform music			☐ Y ☐ N
Have a water gun fight/ snowball fight			☐ Y ☐ N
Laugh at funny jokes/tell others funny stories			☐ Y ☐ N
Dance around your kitchen			☐ Y ☐ N
Participate in an improv class			☐ Y ☐ N
Take a writing class			☐ Y ☐ N
Watch movies			☐ Y ☐ N
Play pretend or make believe (yes, you can still do this even though you are an adult)			☐ Y ☐ N
			☐ Y ☐ N
			☐ Y ☐ N
			☐ Y ☐ N
			☐ Y ☐ N
			☐ Y ☐ N
			☐ Y ☐ N

Chapter 5

FINDING EQUANIMITY IN ANY STORM

Every moment of equanimity is a moment of waking up from the delusion that things should be as we want them to be.

—Toni Bernhard

As you may have gathered, perspective is almost everything when strengthening one's resilience. The power of perspective can help us undo toxic, unhelpful narratives and create more opportunities to have healthier and happier lives.

EXERCISE

To reiterate the power of perspective, consider the statement below:

YOUARENOWHERE

Without too much overthinking, when you see the above letters, what do they say?

....

Reread the same lines and come up with some other ways it can be interpreted.

....

....

....

As you may have guessed, the letters YOUARENOWHERE have two different interpretations, and you have a choice about how you want to interpret it: "You are nowhere" OR "You are now here."

Take a quick moment to reflect on how you initially perceived the letters YOUARENOWHERE. Check in with your body and see how it feels when you think of the other way this statement can be read. Again, check in with your body and notice how it feels.

Ask yourself if it is more helpful to choose a more optimistic or pessimistic way of thought.

TYPES OF RESILIENT THINKING

Often, when people are asked to do this exercise and to think about the more positive interpretation of this statement, "You are now here," they describe a sensation of fullness, optimism, and hopefulness compared to when they reflect on their feelings regarding the other interpretation, "You are nowhere." The truth is that building our resilience is not only about reframing an old narrative or kicking negative thoughts from our mind. It often includes choices about what we decide to think and how it makes us feel.

While the workbook provides several ways of reframing negative thoughts into positive thoughts, note that how you choose to think applies to both micro-moments and macro levels. For instance, your overall thinking style significantly impacts your levels of resilience. This makes sense as someone less hopeful may often experience more negative thoughts and psycho-social barriers, such as poor mental state, anxiety, apprehension, and low self-esteem, preventing them from moving forward.

Take the case of Amanda.

CASE SCENARIO

Amanda and her family had migrated to the US from Guinea when she was 10. When she and her family lived in Guinea, they were privileged; however, this did not exempt Amanda from female genital mutilation. As a result, Amanda's parents decided to relocate to the US for a safer experience for their daughters and the hope of new opportunities. There was nothing easy in Amanda and her family's migration experience to the US. Amanda's parents could not transfer their professional skills to employment here. The family had to live in a one-bedroom apartment for a few years before they felt financial security.

Despite such hardship, Amanda recounted that she and her family held a sense of optimism, patience, and hope that the next day would be better. Amanda shared that this "tomorrow will be better" mantra almost always held, noting that it likely had something to do with her family's gratitude practice. Growing up, her family had ritualized this gratitude practice so that no matter what disappointing or challenging thing happened during the day, each member of the family would highlight something positive, even if it was something small. They highlighted the fact that something good could happen every day.

Amanda's sense of hope and optimism for her future were apparent. In many ways, Amanda shared that maintaining a world view of hope and optimism was her survival strategy. Such an ability to focus on the bright spots in the future allowed Amanda to have a greater capacity to be patient and flexible as she became familiar with American culture, navigated the public school system, and later pursued college and higher education.

POSITIVITY AND OPTIMISM

The vignette of Amanda exemplifies how different types of thinking can foster and enhance one's resiliency. For instance, we notice that Amanda's sense of positivity—her ability to focus on what feels good in the moment—supported her through difficult days, while her sense of optimism—her outlook on events in her life—helped her achieve her goals. It seems that early on, Amanda and her family were onto a secret about resiliency that more and more researchers in the field have taken decades to learn—that when we focus on the stuff that is working, more and more we start to see things go in our favor.

Historically, researchers and clinicians have focused on identifying what is not working for a person instead of highlighting positives, hoping this leads to a healing path. However, more research indicates that this may not be helpful because it may reinforce negative narratives and strengthen the neurological pathways associated with those unhelpful thought patterns.[58] A newer field of psychology called positive psychology suggests the exact opposite, noting that one's resilience is enhanced when there is a focus on the "good stuff," or the stuff that is working. A core component of positive psychology is that there must be some balance and realism to it. For instance, healthy optimists will maintain a positive outlook while understanding the reality of the situation and radically accepting the outcome if they try to accomplish their goal. Understandably, positivity comes with practice, just as in the case of Amanda. The more you practice positivity, the more it will strengthen positive neurological connections and, hopefully, bring you more happiness and resilience.

---

58 Deborah Ross and Kathleen Adams, *Your Brain on Ink: A Workbook on Neuroplasticity and the Journal Ladder* (Lanham, MD: Rowman & Littlefield, 2016).

Positive affirmations can go a long way in rewiring strong negative narratives or thoughts about ourselves or our daily experiences. Sometimes when we hit a rut, a friendly reminder is just what we need.

Some of us may already have a list of positive affirmations that we reference; however, below is a list that may be helpful to you.

- I trust myself and my inner wisdom.
- I am a kind, compassionate person.
- I am generous.
- I am valued.
- I am successful and productive.

- No matter the outcome, I will be okay and will persevere.
- I dare to overcome this obstacle.
- Nothing is permanent.
- This, too, shall pass.

For this exercise, list five positive affirmations you might want to say to yourself or remind yourself of daily. You can use the above list as a guide or create affirmations that resonate with you.

1.
2.
3.
4.
5.

Once you have determined what affirmations will help you, keep them on your person (e.g., in your pocket or bag) or around places you frequent. Some people like to have a list in their pocket or on their phones so they can quickly access them when they need a boost. Others find it helpful to list these affirmations on sticky notes strewn around their home, workplace, or car. One former client had affirmations posted above her light switches, in mirrors, and by her computer.

EXERCISE

While affirmations help us stop negative thought patterns and stay in the moment, cultivating a greater sense of optimism will allow us to change our overall schema and the way we see the world. As demonstrated earlier, most of us who approach the world optimistically have more favorable mental and physical health outcomes.

For this exercise, do your best to use your imagination and visualize different scenarios—one as an optimist and another as a pessimist. The first step in this exercise is to channel and embrace the persona of a pessimist. You may first want to close your eyes and imagine stepping into the shoes of a pessimistic person you know in real life or in fiction.

For instance, you may want to imagine putting yourself in the shoes of Angela Martin from *The Office* or April Ludgate from *Parks and Recreation*, two of television's greatest pessimists. While embracing such characters' personas and your own lived experiences, how do you imagine you would answer the following questions from their perspective?

What were some of the negative emotions that came up for you this week?

....

....

....

Name some things that caused you to become frustrated or irritable this week.

....

....

....

Reflect on some of the challenges you faced on a personal and professional level.

....

....

....

What are some things that resulted in you feeling disappointed in yourself this week?

....

....

....

Now for the second part of the exercise, imagine putting yourself in the shoes of an optimist, for instance Leslie Knope from *Parks and Recreation* or Kimmy Schmidt from *The Unbreakable Kimmy Schmidt*. As you did above, imagine embracing these characters' personas and how you would answer the following questions from the perspective of an optimist. Evaluate how you would see the events of this past week from a positive lens and then answer the following questions.

What were some of the positive emotions that came up for you this week?

Name some things that caused you to become happy, excited, or joyful this week.

Reflect on some of the achievements you experienced on a personal and professional level.

What are some things that resulted in you feeling proud of yourself this week?

Evaluate the questions below having experienced what life might look like from both an optimist's and pessimist's perspective. Reflect on the following questions.

What was it like to embody the pessimistic mindset?

What was it like to embody the optimistic mindset?

Which mask was or would be easier to wear?

_____

_____

_____

What did you learn from this exercise?

_____

_____

_____

How could you put into action what you learned from this exercise?

_____

_____

_____

EXERCISE

Amanda always had something to look toward, whether she was aware of it or not. When it is hard to muster the motivation to be optimistic, creating a vision board can be helpful. The purpose of a vision board is twofold: 1.) to spur positive thinking in the moment, and 2.) to help you achieve your longer-term goals. While some are skeptical about whether vision boards are helpful, research indicates that they help people start to dream about their futures, stimulating different, likely more positive, neurological connections in the brain.[59] This makes it more likely for us to engage in positive habits that are moving us toward our goals.

To create your vision board, you can follow the below steps. Remember that a vision board is about your vision. There is no clear right or wrong way to make one. However, keep in mind that the secret to an impactful vision board is to fill it exclusively with images and words that promote an optimistic mindset.

Step 1: Visualize your objectives or the things you are optimistic about in real life.

Step 2: Collect images, quotes, or other items that symbolize what you want for yourself or that you find inspirational.

---

59 Daniel L. Schacter et al., "The Future of Memory: Remembering, Imagining, and the Brain," _Neuron_ 76, no. 4 (November 2012): 677–94, https://doi.org/10.1016/j.neuron.2012.11.001.

Step 3: On a poster board, assemble the respective images, quotes, and words to your liking.

Step 4: Place the completed vision board where you can notice it every day.

Step 5: Revise and reimagine the vision board as needed and as desired.

POSITIVITY + OPTIMISM = HOPEFULNESS

Combining a positive mindset with optimism can increase levels of resilience and, as a result, serve as a protective factor against one's subjective experience of hardship. In this context, hope is one's ability to expect the best in the future and motivation to achieve goals. Research has found that hopeful individuals don't get stopped when they encounter adversity; instead, they use their optimism and brainstorm ways to overcome challenges. Individuals who are high in hope not only have more resiliency when overcoming physical ailments, including life-threatening ones, but tend to demonstrate more efficacy in other areas of their life, such as athletics, profession, and academics.[60] The research indicates a direct, inverse relationship between hopefulness and depression.[61]

The science of hope explains why thinking about the future positively is a huge determinant of our overall personal and professional success. Have you ever noticed that when you see a direct correlation between the future you want and your behaviors/actions, you begin to engage in behaviors that align with the goal you want to achieve? This is true for most of us—when we are committed to achieving a goal, we either consciously or unconsciously work toward it.

Traditionally, goal setting would solely rely on willpower to achieve a specific goal. Think of the SMART goal model. In this model, goals need to be Specific, Measurable, Achievable, Relevant, and Timely. The aim of this mode is to break down one large goal into several smaller pieces. The hope is that by piecemealing the goals you will save enough willpower to achieve the desired outcome. In hope theory, dreams are accomplished not only by willpower but also by way power.[62] Way power, in this case, is best defined as the actual path to completing the goal, which accounts for the obstacles you may encounter. Remember that another feature of hope is believing in yourself enough to overcome an obstacle. Hope researchers believe that pursuing the goal is almost as vital to overall well-being as achieving it.[63]

60 Luthans et al., "The Development and Resulting Performance Impact of Positive Psychological Capital."

61 Devika Duggal, Amanda Sacks-Zimmerman, and Taylor Liberta, "The Impact of Hope and Resilience on Multiple Factors in Neurosurgical Patients," Cureus, October 26, 2016, https://doi.org/10.7759/cureus.849.

62 C. R. Snyder, *Handbook of Hope: Theory, Measures and Applications* (San Diego: Academic Press, 2000).

63 Snyder, *Handbook of Hope: Theory, Measures and Applications;* Sonja Lyubomirsky, *The How of Happiness: A Practical Guide to Getting the Life You Want* (London: Piatkus, 2013).

EXERCISE

Who wouldn't benefit from just a bit more hopefulness? I doubt that there are many naysaysers to this proposition. Researchers on hopefulness suggest that hope as a state of being is a belief and a feeling and can be quantified into four components—action, options, evidence, and connection.[64] Hope has a strong influence on the desired outcomes of a person and can be assessed along a continuum of "no hope" to "high hope." Answer yes or no to the questions within each of the four domains of hope to get a better sense of how hopeful you are.

	STATEMENT	YES/NO
ACTIONS	I feel as though I have enough energy to pursue my goals.	
	I do my best not to let negative thoughts get in my way of achieving my goals.	
	My past experiences have allowed me to persevere.	
	I feel efficacious.	
	I can see the path toward what I hope to accomplish.	
OPTIONS	I can think of ways to get out of a tough situation.	
	I believe that there are many ways to solve difficult problems.	
	I don't feel as though I have an option to give up on myself.	
	I don't often worry about things that aren't in my control.	
	I am willing to do whatever it takes to achieve what I desire.	
EVIDENCE	I have been able to overcome several difficult experiences from my past.	
	I try not to let naysayers get in my way of achieving my dreams.	
	Others are impressed by my success.	
	I believe that if I work hard and put in the effort to change a situation it will be okay.	
	When I look back at my life, I am surprised by how much I have accomplished.	

---

64 C. R. Snyder, "Conceptualizing, Measuring, and Nurturing Hope," *Journal of Counseling & Development* 73, no. 3 (January 2, 1995): 355–60, https://doi.org/10.1002/j.1556-6676.1995.tb01764.x.

	STATEMENT	YES/NO
CONNECTION	I have supports around me who believe that I can get through tough situations.	
	Even when those around me feel discouraged, I can move forward.	
	Others look up to me for guidance/counsel.	
	I feel motivated by feedback from my community support.	
	I believe in a higher power.	
	Total Answers of Yes	

Now, score the number of statements you answered yes to and assess where they fall along the continuum of hope.

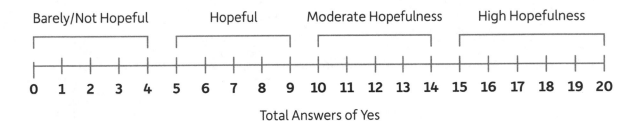

Higher scores reflect more hope. You can revisit this assessment to measure your levels of hope over time. If you are someone who scored lower, don't worry, it is important to note that hope is fluid and flexible and does move along a continuum (meaning that hope is always changing).

If you are interested in building and sustaining more hope, you may benefit from participating in therapy or by exploring some of the strategies below.

HOPE-BUILDING STRATEGIES

1. Focus on what IS working in your life. Even if it is low-hanging fruit, acknowledge and honor the good stuff.
2. Stay in your own lane. Focus on yourself and do your best to ignore what others are doing—falling prey to social media posts where people are curating their feeds can add to a cycle of negativity.
3. Get some good cheerleaders. Find a mentor, a friend, a colleague, an intimate other who believes in you and can offer you encouragement when it feels like all hope is lost.

4. Mentally examine your "best" and "worst case" scenarios. By naming the best and worst case scenarios, you are allowing yourself to have agency even if the outcome isn't what you had wanted.

5. Look for awe-inspiring moments. Finding the awe in life allows us to recognize our limited power and can remind us that anything is possible.

6. Develop a spiritual connection/community, which for some can be calming, meditative, and connecting.

7. Look for hope models or mentors. In times of tremendous difficulty it can be helpful to look to and speak to someone who has had similar struggles and see how they were able to persevere through difficult times.

EXERCISE

Identifying, naming, and achieving your hopes can be challenging, especially in the immediate face of adversity. This exercise will help you identify your hopes and find a path.

Given your current circumstance and whatever you are up against, what are you hoping for now?

_____

_____

_____

_____

Why is this hope important to you?

_____

_____

_____

_____

If you decide to embrace this hope, how is it helping you get to your longer-term goals?

_____

_____

_____

_____

_____

Who or what may be able to help you overcome obstacles that may interfere with you achieving this hope?

_____

_____

_____

_____

_____

_____

EXERCISE

Now that you have identified at least one hope that you would like to come to fruition, you will now work more strategically on your roadmap to a more hopeful, brighter future. Your Hope Plan will help you identify pathways and overcome obstacles that may inhibit hope along your way.

Before you start your Hope Plan, it may be helpful to review how to set goals using the SMART method. Using this method, goals need to be:

Specific: Clearly define your goal. Consider the reason why you are reading this book now. What are you hoping to obtain?

Measurable: Determine how you will measure your goal before starting out. In this instance, your hope/objective may be taking action on a step or exploring options for moving forward. Having something quantifiable will help in measuring progress.

Achievable: Set realistic and attainable goals. For instance, if you are reading this workbook to help you overcome a breakup, you might consider one goal to be getting your ex back etc., but a more realistic goal might be no longer having ruminating thoughts about your time together.

Relevant: Align with your goal. For instance, if you wish to move on from the loss of a significant other, then your goal/hope needs to reflect this. It wouldn't make too much sense if you were working on your grief but you had a goal to move quickly through the stages of grief, which might not be therapeutic or authentic.

Timely: Set a time limit for your goal. While setting a goal in some circumstances, such as in bereavement, might seem antithetical, it is okay to set time frames when working toward achieving the smaller goals related to the grieving (e.g., having an expectation that three months after your loss you will be able to journal about your feelings).

Look at Kaya's Hope Plan. Note that like the SMART method, your Hope plan must be realistic, as we know a challenging emotion like grief may come and go.

Kaya's Hope Plan: To overcome the recent passing away of her mother.

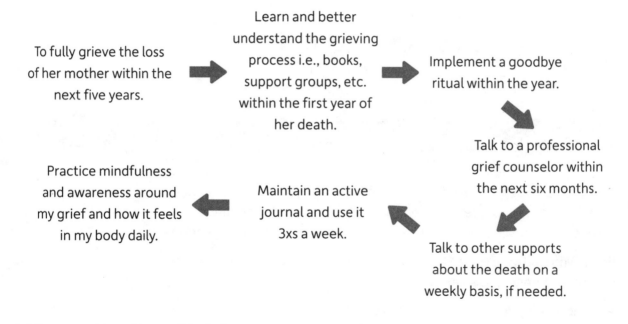

To fully grieve the loss of her mother within the next five years.

Learn and better understand the grieving process i.e., books, support groups, etc. within the first year of her death.

Implement a goodbye ritual within the year.

Talk to a professional grief counselor within the next six months.

Talk to other supports about the death on a weekly basis, if needed.

Maintain an active journal and use it 3xs a week.

Practice mindfulness and awareness around my grief and how it feels in my body daily.

While no two Hope Plans will look the same, it is important to also identify some of the obstacles that may interrupt your path along with some of the things that may motivate you to go forward when it gets hard. Consider completing the list of obstacles and motivators below. See examples from Kaya's list below. When noting motivators, feel free to use words of affirmation or inspiration quotes. You may even want to insert them on the edges of your Hope Plan if things start to feel especially difficult.

OBSTACLES	MOTIVATORS
The overwhelming sensation of grief.	Nothing is permanent. This feeling of grief will go away.
Having few people who understand the grief.	Looking toward those that have experienced a similar grief and hearing their narratives.

EXERCISE

A popular exercise related to building hope is to write a letter to yourself describing your hopes and why they are important. The intent of this letter is not only to help you solidify your commitment to your hopes and to help you envision how you might feel when they come true, but to also come up with a realistic time frame to accomplish them. When you have completed the letter to yourself, seal it, then either ask someone else to mail it to you in the future or email it yourself (you may want to auto-send it later).

Chapter 6

TO GO FORWARD, YOU MUST GROW

When we are no longer able to change a situation—we are challenged to change ourselves.

—Viktor Frankl

As you near completing this workbook, it may be evident that so much of increasing your resilience is about shifting your mindset or the frames in which you previously saw the world. Considering ways to manage stress, deconstruct and reconstruct your narrative, hold a sense of optimism and hope, and reframe negative thoughts, it sure seems that resilience relies more on nurture than nature. This notion that if you water your resilience, it can grow is very hopeful yet challenging.

A former client likened resilience building during a crisis to his experience of the draft during Vietnam—drafting young men who didn't know much about the war while telling them to fight for their lives (and others'). Perhaps this person's analogy was slightly aggrandized, but it points out that it is tough to be resilient when adversity is staring you in the face. Yet, like many young soldiers sent off to battle and constantly reassessing their moves, resilience also requires tremendous flexibility—at times, both physical and mental.

Most of the exercises in this workbook give you options for how you want to manage a situation, because the key to resilience is being flexible. When faced with an external dilemma or a tragedy, our initial inclination is to try to "fix" the problem; however, there are at times so many external factors beyond our control that we might have to be flexible and roll with whatever happens next. Interestingly, resilience research posits that people with higher levels of resiliency are not only those who can be flexible with events shifting but can also shift their affective (psychological state, mood, and emotions) and physiological responses so that they match the new outcome.[65] The gist is that more flexible people tend to be adaptable to examining things from multiple perspectives so that they can choose how to respond. The next case scenario of a fictional character exemplifies this.

---

[65] Christian E. Waugh, Renee J. Thompson, and Ian H. Gotlib, "Flexible Emotional Responsiveness in Trait Resilience," *Emotion* 11, no. 5 (2011): 1059–67, https://doi.org/10.1037/a0021786.

CASE SCENARIO

One of the best examples of the benefits of flexibility is demonstrated by Diane Lane's character, Frances Mayes, in the 2003 film *Under the Tuscan Sun*. The film's plot follows Frances as she learns that her husband is cheating on her, and her life gets turned upside down. Unable to regulate her emotions and self-soothe around her recent divorce, Frances falls into a deep depression. Her dear friend encourages her to take her place on a group tour of Tuscany. With much prodding, Frances embarks on a tour to find herself deeply enamored with a particular villa. She impulsively decides that she will buy this villa and stay in this remote community. After many trials and tribulations—from learning how to navigate a foreign country, being single, and figuring out how to remodel a villa—Frances adapts to her new life. There is a pivotal moment in the film where Frances reminisces about her hopes for herself. She becomes teary and tells a local how she wants to have children, a wedding in her house, and a new lover. The local pauses Frances and, in the screenshot, highlights how she has all these things—a child, a wedding, and a lover—but not how Frances envisioned it coming together for herself. The moral of this story is that once Frances starts to be flexible, things begin to come together as she wants.

EXERCISE

Most of us are often flexible without even noticing. Like the concept of radical acceptance, being flexible, especially in a crisis, can be challenging, and as a result, practice can be helpful. Below are some tips for practicing mental and emotional stability to build up more capacity.

1. Try to keep your mind stimulated every day with something new. *Learn a new skill or a word. Play a puzzle.*

2. Do something different and do that often. *Try changing your routine and building new neural pathways.*

3. Engage in different activities. *Try drinking Sprite instead of Coke. Try mountain climbing instead of running.*

4. Get out of your comfort zone. *Give yourself a challenge by engaging in a new and mildly stressful activity.*

5. Stay present. *Be in the here and now despite whatever else is occurring.*

6. Stay emotionally open. *Allow yourself to experience all the thoughts and feelings that arise when they do.*

7. Participate in therapy. *Explore your past experiences with difficult situations and how you responded to them.*

8. Practice mindfulness. *Work to slow your nervous system down and be more connected to yourself.*

MINDFULNESS

If flexibility is at the core of resilience, then mindfulness is its outer shell. Closely associated with meditation, mindfulness allows us to focus on the present moment and be flexible, and can differentiate between our emotional experience of a situation and reality. For instance, if you are mindful or more aware, you can tell when you are having a bad day and what its origin is versus just feeling like you are in a funk.

Mindfulness is something we all possess; however, it is easier to access with more regular practice. Research has indicated that those who set aside time to engage in a mindfulness practice benefit from stress relief/reduction, self-control, and mental clarity, among other rewards. Many start their mindfulness practice using meditation, which focuses on breathwork to help you move to the present moment without getting caught up in thoughts, emotions, and sounds. The goal of meditation is to bring you back to the moment to help you notice things, such as your breath and what is happening to you somatically; it can be a helpful tool to access mindfulness daily.

EXERCISE

Regardless of your experience with meditation, the exercise below is a simple and easy meditation that anyone can utilize.

Step 1: Find a solid, sturdy seat. Sit on it however you please, so long as you feel comfortable.

Step 2: Once you are comfortable, you can either close your eyes or find a focal point in the room where you can lower your gaze.

Step 3: Set your timer for one minute.

Step 4: Start by inhaling and breathing to the count of 4. Hold your breath for a count of 7, and exhale to hear the swoosh of air releasing for a count of 8.

Step 5: Focus on the inhale and exhale of your breath. Do your best to hold your attention and try not to focus on any thoughts or feelings that arise. If they arise, don't worry; do your best to redirect your attention to your breath. Let go of any judgment or criticism that you may encounter.

Step 6: Continue inhaling and exhaling until the time is up.

Step 7: When the timer goes off, open your eyelids or gently lift your gaze.

Step 8: Take a moment to notice any sensations or energy in your body. Notice any sounds in the environment. Notice your thoughts or emotions.

Step 9: Assess if this exercise was easy or hard for you. What was the hardest part of this exercise? What was the easiest part? Would you consider doing this type of meditation on your own?

EXERCISE

Now that you have tried a simple meditation, try a mindfulness activity. You will need either a lukewarm cup of water or tea for this activity. Please be mindful that you will be sipping the liquid in this exercise, so it mustn't be too hot.

Many people use tea-sipping as an act of mindfulness if they are particularly anxious and cannot complete a full meditation. The goal of this exercise is to slow down, pause, and savor the moment with a splendid cup of tea.

Taking direction from Buddhist priest Thich Nhat Hanh, we plan to use these pauses for sitting in the momentary silence they offer. When Thich Nhat Hanh would conduct a mindfulness practice in front of his followers, he would often take a dramatic pause when pouring his tea and taking the first sip; he would slowly raise the cup to his lips and enjoy slow sips of the tea. He would hold the cup with both hands to demonstrate that his entire focus was on the tea—nothing else. Thich Nhat Hanh's intentionality with the tea reflected that he was slowing down and not rushing to the next thing. His disengagement from everything around him allowed him to have a deeper connection with himself and show up more authentically.

Try your tea-sipping mindful activity.

Step 1: Choose a tea to match your mood.

Step 2: Start to boil the water.

Step 3: When the kettle is ready, pour the water into the cup with the tea bag.

Step 4: Watch the tea diffuse through water.

Step 5: When the tea is ready, take a slow sip.

Step 6: Close your eyes and feel the lukewarm water move around your mouth, down your trachea, and into your stomach. Focus on the warmth of the liquid as it moves through your body.

Step 7: Continue this process until there is no more tea.

Step 8: Once you have completely consumed the tea, check in with your body. How are you feeling? Do you notice any energy or sensations moving around? Do you see anything shift in your attention?

GRATITUDE

Gratitude plays a prominent role in your resiliency and how you view the world. Additionally, fostering gratitude can be very useful in promoting a sense of positivity in your daily life. While having a greater understanding of positivity will not stop challenges from occurring, having more buoyancy can make moving through tough times more manageable. The research on gratitude posits that actively practicing gratitude, whether it is a daily reflection of things you are grateful for or taking a moment to acknowledge the good stuff, correlates with your self-control.[66] Consider the cases of trauma survivors who can express gratitude despite their pain, feeling that their experience has enriched their lives somehow. While this is not universally true of all trauma survivors, for many, talking about traumatic experiences helps to achieve a sense of agency over their circumstances and their narrative.

Angela was one such survivor.

CASE SCENARIO

Angela was two years old when she experienced significant burns on her face, limbs, and torso. Her father tried to burn her and her mother to prevent them from leaving him. Angela spent most of her young childhood in and out of hospital rooms to manage the pain and physical scarring. As an adult, Angela decided to flip the script. For her, this meant talking about the tremendous impact this trauma had on her and her decision to become a fitness instructor and dancer. Angela faced the difficulty of managing physical therapy as a young person while trying to fit in. She experienced incongruence just looking into the mirror and seeing a face that she did not feel fit her.

A few years ago, Angela received a modeling contract, launching her professional training career into the spotlight. A large part of Angela's message to other survivors of domestic violence is her gratitude for what her body can do, such as being a mother, instructor, partner, and advocate. Angela often shares how her life would have been very different without this trauma, and even in her most painful moments, she shares that she would not have chosen anything different. A core component of Angela's mission is to help others heal and dose out random acts of kindness, which she calls *mitzvahs*, the Yiddish word for "good deeds."

---

66 Fernanda Inéz García-Vázquez, Angel Alberto Valdés-Cuervo, and Lizeth Guadalupe Parra-Pérez, "The Effects of Forgiveness, Gratitude, and Self-Control on Reactive and Proactive Aggression in Bullying," *International Journal of Environmental Research and Public Health* 17, no. 16 (August 10, 2020): 5760, https://doi.org/10.3390/ijerph17165760.

EXERCISE

For practice in gratitude to be meaningful, it goes beyond just saying thank you. It needs to be intentional and specific. Many of us only acknowledge the big things, but it is just as important to notice and recognize the more minor things. To continue your work on building your gratitude practice, try the following ideas:

1. Consider keeping a gratitude journal.
2. Consider reflecting on the following prompts for at least five consecutive days, dedicating a specific time of the day—morning or night—when you can commit to the reflection. (Hint: You may want to photocopy this exercise and review it each day.)

Identify one reason why you are glad that you woke up today.

....

....

Highlight one small but significant thing that evoked a sense of happiness.

....

....

Name one act of kindness that you did for someone else. Name an act of kindness that someone did for you.

....

....

Name one thing that you found inspiring today.

....

....

Name one thing that you are looking forward to tomorrow.

....

....

Do your best to avoid repeating any answers for five days.

....

....

CULTIVATING LOVING KINDNESS AND COMPASSION

Whenever I am the recipient of a random act of kindness, I have a tremendous amount of appreciation and gratitude, and I feel a sense of warmth and community. Such an experience has enough energy to change what could have been a downright awful day to one full of light and energy. The joy and happiness you experience when you either give or receive an act of kindness can be expansive. Those positive feelings can be powerful enough to transcend grief, loss, jealousy, or other negative emotions.

Amanda Gilbert, author of *Kindness Now,* suggests that the joy or "elevation" that we experience when we see unexpected acts of human kindness and goodness opens our hearts, allowing us to nurture ourselves.[67] Perhaps our hearts open as we see ourselves being more connected and empathetic to others, reminding us of our power, purpose, and agency.

When giving or receiving acts of kindness or compassion, we have an emotional experience that allows for greater and deeper awareness and acceptance of ourselves.[68] Such experiences promote mindful self-compassion—a concept developed by compassion researchers Chris Germer at Harvard University and Kristen Neff at the University of Texas, Austin. The premise behind mindful self-compassion is twofold. The first step is being aware of what is causing your suffering, and then, with loving awareness, turning toward your pain. The second component of self-compassion is the notion suffering is part of the shared human experience and is something that we all go through as opposed to something that simply happens to the individual. When taken together, mindful self-compassion means allowing yourself to be aware of your complicated feelings and approaching your emotions in a warm, loving, soothing, compassionate manner—remembering that you are human, after all.

Consider the case of Jenna.

CASE SCENARIO

Jenna, a recent newlywed, had relocated with her spouse and her children to a suburb outside her hometown. For the first few months of marriage, Jenna could not have been happier preparing her new home, starting a new job, and integrating with her new stepchildren. Everything seemed hunky-dory until, just before Jenna began speaking at a large work meeting, she received a text from a friend stating that she had noticed Jenna's wife on a singles' dating app. Shocked, Jenna's amygdala went into overdrive. Without having any awareness of what was happening, Jenna stormed out of the conference room into her car.

---

67 Amanda Gilbert, *Kindness Now: A 28-Day Guide to Living with Authenticity, Intention, and Compassion* (Boulder, CO: Shambhala, 2021).

68 Kristin Neff, *Self-Compassion: The Proven Power of Being Kind to Yourself* (London: Yellow Kite, an imprint of Hodder & Stoughton, 2021).

She was dumbfounded and spent the next several hours cycling through feelings of disbelief, shock, anger, and sadness. Later that evening, Jenna went home and straight to bed. Jenna was a barely functional version of her past self for the next two weeks. She could not return her manager's or colleagues' phone calls and fell into depression. Not only was Jenna deeply pained by her wife's betrayal, but she was also humiliated by her actions at work. Jenna contemplated the pros and the cons of sharing this information with her manager, hoping that there would be some understanding and compassion for her current situation.

After about a week, Jenna had to make some changes. Indeed, her situation at home was not going to be resolved overnight, and she needed to return to her work. In our sessions, the work focused on Jenna making sense of this betrayal and cultivating greater compassion for her situation. Utilizing a technique derived from Gramer and Neff, *treating yourself like your own best friend,* I asked Jenna to consider what advice she would give a friend in the same case. Then, I asked Jenna to think about befriending herself in the same way. What would it feel like to take some of her advice? She did just that. The morning following our session, Jenna spoke to her manager and asked if she could use some of her PTO as she sorted out her home situation. Jenna's manager was sympathetic, and upon returning to work, Jenna learned that her manager had experienced something similar, an excellent reminder to Jenna that practice in mindful self-compassion can go a long way.

EXERCISE

If you are working on building more self-compassion, a good place to start is the concept of loving kindness. The concept of loving kindness is being a gentle friend to yourself regardless of what is happening in the moment. Loving kindness refers to having an open heart with the wish and motivation for oneself along with others to be happy. Although the concept of loving kindness or metta is rooted in Buddhism, its value is supported by quantum physics, which purports that thoughts and our words have energy that is transmitted within and between each one of us.[69] Thus, angry thoughts promote anger and love begets love.

If you are familiar with metta meditation, you understand that the person who has let go of negativity finds themselves more likely to be surrounded by loving thoughts, loving people, loving events, etc.

For this exercise, I want you to reflect upon a recent unpleasant exchange or event. Consider the example of if you were walking down the street and a bicyclist accidentally side swipes you. Perhaps your first, automatic thought is *What a jerk!* Consider how that negative exchange may impact your mood for the rest of the day. Now consider if you were to respond to this incident with loving kindness—maybe your automatic response is something like, *Wow, they must be in a rush* or *Maybe*

---

69 Hawkins, *Letting Go: The Pathway of Surrender.*

they are having a bad day. How might that response shift your energy and mood for the rest of the day?

Jot down a recent negative interaction with someone.

How do you remember responding to the situation?

How did that experience make you feel for the rest of the day?

How did you offer yourself compassion in that moment?

Were you able to offer the other person compassion? If so, what did it look like?

Now, can you imagine if you had approached that situation with loving kindness? Can you write down what that would look like?

How does using that practice make you feel about the situation now?

How are you able to offer yourself compassion?

Chapter 7
LOOKING AHEAD

Congratulations! You are about to end this chapter of your resilience journey and start the next phase. Whether you have slowly worked through the exercises contained in this workbook or selected those most relevant to you, the hope is that you have increased your capacity for restored and adaptive resilience. As promised, we will now revisit one of the first exercises of this book to compare the progress you have made from start to finish.

EXERCISE

Just as you did when you started this workbook, review each of the items listed below and rank them on a 5-point scale ranging from 1 to 5, with 1 being strongly disagree and 5 being strongly agree.

STATEMENT	STRONGLY DISAGREE	DISAGREE	NEUTRAL	AGREE	STRONGLY AGREE
1. I tend to bounce back quickly after hard times.	1	2	3	4	5
2. I have an easy time making it through stressful events.	1	2	3	4	5
3. It does not take me long to recover from a stressful event.	1	2	3	4	5
4. It is easy for me to snap back when something bad happens.	1	2	3	4	5

STATEMENT	STRONGLY DISAGREE	DISAGREE	NEUTRAL	AGREE	STRONGLY AGREE
5. I usually come through difficult times with little trouble.	1	2	3	4	5
6. I tend to take a short time to get over setbacks in my life.	1	2	3	4	5
My Score (Sum ÷ 6)					

Add the numbers up and assess how they compare to your assessment at the start of the workbook. Remember that the total possible score ranges from 1 to 5, and a higher score correlates to higher levels of resiliency.

How do your scores compare to before you started reviewing the workbook? Did you notice anything shift? Do you feel more confident and in control of where you are headed? Can you be more flexible and adaptable?

Review the exercises as needed if you notice some areas where you need continued support. Practicing will not only reinforce your learning, it will also keep those neurological pathways open. Remember that your mental toughness is at the core of resilience—your ability to be positive, flexible, and optimistic will allow you to persevere through anything. Harnessing your power will allow you to rewrite your story and make new meanings as you encounter new hardships and opportunities along your journey.

Now, let's revisit the questions you answered at the very beginning of the workbook (on page 6) that explored your willingness to grow. How do your answers differ now?

What is the finish line or challenge you are working toward overcoming? How would you feel if it ended differently from how you imagine?

How would you know if you were to be more resilient? What would that look like?

_____

_____

_____

_____

Can you name the scariest part(s) of this journey?

_____

_____

_____

_____

What are you most hopeful about in pursuing this journey?

_____

_____

_____

_____

Remember that even though you have flexed and worked at building your resilience muscles, parts of your journey will at times stir up emotions ranging from efficacy, hopefulness, and joy to sadness, grief, and disappointment. No matter how strong you are, it is essential to recognize and allow all the feelings to come to you. Remember that along all of your journeys, you will have to do a lot of rewriting, and even though you may have to let go of how you thought your life should be, it doesn't mean that it won't be better than you hoped!

Don't be afraid to stand in the discomfort and messiness of life—channel your inner female warrior and use your courage to honor your ancestors who tolerated their pain and challenges so that you could be here today. Good luck and warm wishes!

WORKS CITED

ACE Response—Adverse Childhood Experiences, ACEs, ACE Response, Restorative Integral Support, RIS. Accessed April 2, 2023. https://www.cdc.gov/violenceprevention/aces/index.html.

Burns, David D. *Feeling Good: The New Mood Therapy*. New York, NY: Avon Books, 1999.

Deborah Ross and Kathleen Adams. *Your Brain on Ink: A Workbook on Neuroplasticity and the Journal Ladder*. Lanham, MD: Rowman & Littlefield, 2016.

Diamond, Marian Cleeves. *Enriching Heredity: The Impact of the Environment on the Anatomy of the Brain*. London: Collier Macmillan, 1988.

Frankl, Viktor E., Harold S. Kushner, and William J. Winslade. *Man's Search for Meaning*. Boston, MA: Beacon Press, 2006.

Gilbert, Amanda. *Kindness Now: A 28-Day Guide to Living with Authenticity, Intention, and Compassion*. Boulder, CO: Shambhala, 2021.

Goldstein, Elisha. *Uncovering Happiness: Overcoming Depression with Mindfulness and Self-Compassion*. New York: Atria Books, 2016.

Hawkins, David R. *Letting Go: The Pathway of Surrender*. Carlsbad, CA: Hay House, Inc., 2018.

Hone, Lucy, and Karen Reivich. *Resilient Grieving: How to Find Your Way through a Devastating Loss*. New York, NY: The Experiment, 2017.

Ikigai Living. "Ikigai: The Japanese Answer to a Life of Purpose." Accessed March 12, 2023. https://ikigai-living.com/what-is-ikigai.

Ivtzan, Itai, Piers Worth, Kate Hefferon, and Tim Lomas. *Second Wave Positive Psychology: Embracing the Dark Side of Life*. London, United Kingdom: Routledge, 2016.

Lieberman, Matthew D. *Social: Why Our Brains Are Wired to Connect*. Oxford (GB): Oxford University Press, 2015.

Lyubomirsky, Sonja. *The How of Happiness: A Practical Guide to Getting the Life You Want*. London: Piatkus, 2013.

Neff, Kristin. *Self-Compassion: The Proven Power of Being Kind to Yourself*. London: Yellow Kite, an imprint of Hodder & Stoughton, 2021.

van der Kolk, Bessel. *The Body Keeps the Score: Mind, Brain and Body in the Transformation of Trauma*. UK: Penguin Books, 2015.

Wolin, Steven J., and Sybil Wolin. *The Resilient Self: How Survivors of Troubled Families Rise above Adversity*. New York: Villard Books, 1994.

ACKNOWLEDGMENTS

First, and most importantly, I want to thank you, the reader, for taking the chance and choosing this workbook as you move forward on your resilience journey. I realize that many of you may be in a moment of profound suffering and pain, and I hope that this workbook brought you some resolve, comfort, and motivation to continue to persevere.

To all my clients, especially those courageous women, who endlessly demonstrate the power of their own resilience as they move through some of challenging experiences that women today face. I have profound gratitude for you and am honored to have the privilege to watch your journey. Thank you to the two most important women, thus far, in my life—my mother, Linda Kelaher, whose presence and spirit of resilience is missed every day that she is no longer with us, and to my grandmother, Catherine Harosinko, who gave me unconditional love and support as I struggled with anxiety as a teenager.

To my professional mentors, colleagues, and friends—thank you for always being there. I feel blessed and privileged to know you. Your constant words of encouragement and love have helped strengthen my own confidence to take risks such as writing a book and have the courage to move forward even when there are rocky waters. Specific thanks go to my colleagues Ruthie Israeli and Miriam Denmark, who have offered me continuous support and encouragement. Sydney Reid, you have been such a rock over the last few years. Lastly, to John Dimaras and Kostaki, thank you both for putting up deadlines, long hours, and writing weekends.

I also wish to thank Ulysses Press Staff—Claire Sielaff, Bridget Thoreson, and Renee Rutledge for your patience, hard work, and diligence in making this workbook possible.

ABOUT THE AUTHOR

Hope Kelaher is a therapist based in New York City. She has extensive training in relational and systemic therapy and received postgraduate training from the Ackerman Institute for the Family. Hope has a degree in public health from The Johns Hopkins University and a clinical social work degree from Columbia University. Her passion is helping those struggling with anxiety and depression find solace and connection. Hope currently lives in Manhattan with her partner and her pup, Luna. In her spare time, Hope enjoys long walks with her dog, training for half-marathons, fishing, cooking, and meeting new people.